I0762357

THE ORDER OF PENANCE

THE ROMAN RITUAL

RENEWED BY DECREE OF THE MOST HOLY SECOND ECUMENICAL COUNCIL OF THE VATICAN AND PROMULGATED BY AUTHORITY OF POPE PAUL VI

THE ORDER OF PENANCE

ENGLISH TRANSLATION ACCORDING TO THE TYPICAL EDITION

For Use in the Dioceses of the United States of America

Approved by the United States Conference of Catholic Bishops and Confirmed by the Apostolic See

CATHOLIC BOOK PUBLISHING CORP.
New Jersey
2023

Concordat cum originali:
✠ Leonard P. Blair
Chairman, USCCB Committee on Divine Worship
after review by Rev. Andrew Menke
Executive Director, USCCB Secretariat of Divine Worship

Imprimatur:
✠ Kevin J. Sweeney, D.D.
Bishop of Paterson

October 28, 2022

T-117

ISBN 978-1-958237-09-0

Printed in Korea 23 NT 1

catholicbookpublishing.com

CONTENTS

Decree of the Sacred Congregation for Divine Worship 7

Decree of Confirmation of the Congregation for Divine Worship and the Discipline of the Sacraments 10

Decree of Promulgation of the United States Conference of Catholic Bishops 11

Introduction 13

Chapter I: The Order for Reconciling Individual Penitents 41

Chapter II: The Order for Reconciling Several Penitents with Individual Confession and Absolution 47

Chapter III: The Order for Reconciling Several Penitents with General Confession and Absolution 79

Chapter IV: Various Texts to Be Used in the Celebration of Reconciliation 87

- I. For the Reconciliation of One Penitent.. 89
- II. For the Reconciliation of Several Penitents 101

Appendices

I. Absolution from Censures 265
Dispensation from Irregularity..............266

II. Examples of Penitential Celebrations....267
Preparing Penitential Celebrations......267
I. Penitential Celebrations during Lent 269
II. Penitential Celebration during Advent...................................290
III. Common Penitential Celebrations....................................302
IV. For Children....................................325
V. For Young People.............................330
VI. For the Sick.....................................338

III. Form for the Examination of Conscience...348

SACRED CONGREGATION FOR DIVINE WORSHIP

Prot. n. 800/73

DECREE

Our Lord Jesus Christ brought about reconciliation between God and the human race by the mystery of his Death and Resurrection (cf. Rom 5:10). This ministry of reconciliation was entrusted by the Lord to the Church in the person of the Apostles (2 Cor 5:18ff.). The Church performs this ministry by bringing the good news of salvation to people and by baptizing them in water and in the Holy Spirit (cf. Mt 28:19).

But because of human weakness, it happens that Christians "abandon the love they had at first" (cf. Rev 2:4), and even break off the union of friendship with God by sinning. For this reason, to forgive sins committed after Baptism, the Lord instituted the special Sacrament of Penance (cf. Jn 20:21-23), which the Church has faithfully celebrated down through the ages, in various ways indeed, but preserving its essential elements.

The Second Vatican Council declared: "The rite and formulas for the Sacrament of Penance are to be revised, so that they more clearly express both the nature and effect of the Sacrament."[1] In view of this, the Sacred Congregation for Divine

[1]Second Vatican Council, Constitution on the Sacred Liturgy, *Sacrosanctum Concilium*, no. 72: *Acta Apostolicæ Sedis* 56 (1964), p. 118.

Worship has carefully prepared a new *Ordo Pœnitentiæ*, so that the action of the Sacrament may be more fully understood by the faithful.

In this new *Ordo*, besides *The Order for Reconciling Individual Penitents, The Order for Reconciling Several Penitents* has been prepared, to highlight the communal aspect of the Sacrament. In this instance, individual confession and absolution are inserted into the celebration of the word of God. Furthermore, for special cases, *The Order for Reconciling Several Penitents with General Confession and Absolution*, has been composed, according to the Pastoral Norms concerning the giving of sacramental absolution in a general manner, granted by the Sacred Congregation for the Doctrine of the Faith on June 16, 1972.[2]

The Church is solicitous in calling her faithful to continuous conversion and renewal. Desiring, moreover, that the baptized, who have fallen away after the bath of regeneration, should acknowledge their sins committed against God and neighbor and have true penitence in their heart, and trying to prepare them to celebrate the Sacrament of Penance, the Church exhorts them to attend penitential celebrations from time to time. For this reason this Sacred Congregation has drawn up regulations for such celebrations and proposed examples or models of them, which the Conferences of Bishops may adapt to the needs of their own regions.

[2]Cf. *Acta Apostolicæ Sedis* 64 (1972), pp. 510-514.

Therefore, the Supreme Pontiff PAUL VI has by his authority approved the *Ordo Pœnitentiæ*, prepared by the Sacred Congregation for Divine Worship, and ordered its publication. It is to replace the relevant portions of the Roman Ritual now in use. This *Ordo*, composed in Latin, will come into force immediately upon publication, but those in vernacular languages on the date decreed by the Conferences of Bishops, after they have approved the translations into vernacular languages and after they have received confirmation of the Apostolic See.

All things to the contrary notwithstanding.

From the offices of the Sacred Congregation for Divine Worship, December 2, 1973, the First Sunday of Advent.

BY SPECIAL MANDATE OF THE SUPREME PONTIFF

JEAN Card. VILLOT
Secretary of State

✠ A. BUGNINI
Titular Archbishop of Diocletiana
Secretary of the
Sacred Congregation for Divine Worship

CONGREGATIO DE CULTU DIVINO ET DISCIPLINA SACRAMENTORUM

Prot. n. 460/21

CIVITATUM FŒDERATARUM AMERICÆ SEPTENTRIONALIS

Instante Excellentissimo Domino Iosepho Horatio Gomez, Archepiscopo Angelorum in California, Conferentiæ Episcoporum Civitatum Fœderatarum Americæ Septentrionalis Præside, litteris die 8 septembris 2021 datis, vigore facultatum huic Congregationi a Summo Pontifice FRANCISCO tributarum, textum novæ translationis *anglicæ* partis Ritualis Romani cui titulus est *Ordo Pœnitentiæ*, ab eadem Conferentia Episcoporum ad normam iuris, die 17 mensis iunii anno 2021 approbatum, prout in adiecto exstat exemplari, perlibenter confirmamus.

In textu imprimendo inseratur ex integro hoc Decretum, quo ab Apostolica Sede petita confirmatio conceditur.

Eiusdem insuper textus impressi duo exemplaria ad hanc Congregationem transmittantur.

Contrariis quibuslibet minime obstantibus.

Ex ædibus Congregationis de Cultu Divino et Disciplina Sacramentorum, die 25 aprilis 2022, in festo Sancti Marci, evangelistæ.

✠ ARTURUS ROCHE
Præfectus

✠ VICTORIUS FRANCISCUS VIOLA, O.F.M.
Archepiscopus a Secretis

UNITED STATES CONFERENCE OF CATHOLIC BISHOPS

DECREE OF PROMULGATION

In accord with the norms established by the Holy See, this edition of the *Order of Penance* is declared to be the definitive approved English translation of the *Ordo Pœnitentiæ, editio typica* (1973), and is hereby promulgated by authority of the United States Conference of Catholic Bishops.

The *Order of Penance* was canonically approved for use by the United States Conference of Catholic Bishops on June 17, 2021, and was subsequently confirmed by the Apostolic See by decree of the Congregation for Divine Worship and the Discipline of the Sacraments on April 25, 2022 (Prot. n. 460/21).

This rite may be used in the Liturgy as of Ash Wednesday, February 22, 2023, and its use is obligatory as of April 16, 2023, the Second Sunday of Easter (or of Divine Mercy). From that date forward, no other English translation of the rite may be used in the dioceses of the United States of America.

Given at the General Secretariat of the United States Conference of Catholic Bishops, Washington, DC, on June 24, 2022, the Solemnity of the Most Sacred Heart of Jesus.

✠ José H. Gomez
Archbishop of Los Angeles
President, United States Conference of Catholic Bishops

Rev. Michael J.K. Fuller
General Secretary

ABBA
FATHER

THE ORDER OF PENANCE

INTRODUCTION

I. The Ministry of Reconciliation in the History of Salvation

1. The Father has shown his mercy by reconciling the world to himself in Christ, making peace by the Blood of his Cross, with all things whether on earth or in heaven.[1] The Son of God, made man, dwelt among us so that he might free us from slavery to sin[2] and call us out of darkness into his marvelous light.[3] He therefore began his work on earth by preaching repentance and saying: "Repent, and believe in the Gospel" (Mk 1:15).

This invitation to repentance, which had often been preached by the prophets, prepared our hearts for the coming of the Kingdom of God through the voice of John the Baptist, who came "preaching a baptism of repentance for the forgiveness of sins" (Mk 1:4).

Jesus, however, not only exhorted people to repent so as to leave their sins behind and turn to the Lord with all their heart,[4] but he also welcomed sinners and reconciled them with the Father.[5] In addition, he healed the sick, thus giving a sign of his power to forgive sins.[6] Finally, he himself died for our sins, and rose again for our justification.[7] Furthermore, on the night he was

[1]Cf. 2 Cor 5:18f; Col 1:20.
[2]Cf. Jn 8:34-36.
[3]Cf. 1 Pt 2:9.
[4]Cf. Lk 15.
[5]Cf. Lk 5:20, 27-32; 7:48.
[6]Cf. Mt 9:2-8.
[7]Cf. Rom 4:25.

betrayed, beginning his saving Passion,[8] he instituted the Sacrifice of the New Covenant in his Blood for the forgiveness of sins.[9] After his Resurrection, he sent the Holy Spirit on the Apostles, that they might have power to forgive sins or retain them[10] and might receive the office of preaching repentance and forgiveness of sins to all the nations in his name.[11]

To Peter the Lord had said: "I will give you the keys of the Kingdom of Heaven, and whatever you shall bind on earth, shall be bound in heaven; and whatever you shall loose on earth, shall be loosed in heaven" (Mt 16:19). Obedient to the command of the Lord, on the day of Pentecost, Peter preached the forgiveness of sins through Baptism: "Repent . . . and be baptized, every one of you, in the name of Jesus Christ, for the forgiveness of your sins" (Acts 2:38).[12] Since then, the Church has never failed to call people from sin to conversion, and to reveal the victory of Christ over sin through the celebration of Penance.

2. This victory over sin first shows itself in Baptism, in which the old self is crucified with Christ, that the body of sin may be destroyed and that we should no longer be slaves to sin but, rising again with Christ, we should henceforth live for God.[13] For this reason the Church confesses her faith in "one Baptism for the forgiveness of sins."

In the Sacrifice of the Mass the Passion of Christ is made present, and the body handed over for us and the

[8]Cf. *The Roman Missal*, Eucharistic Prayer III.

[9]Cf. Mt 26:28.

[10]Cf. Jn 20:19-23.

[11]Cf. Lk 24:27.

[12]Cf. Acts 3:19, 26; 17:30.

[13]Cf. Rom 6:4-10.

blood poured out for the forgiveness of sins are again offered to God by the Church for the salvation of the whole world. For in the Eucharist Christ is present and is offered as the "Sacrifice of our reconciliation,"[14] so that we, through his Holy Spirit, "may be gathered into one."[15]

But in addition, our Savior Jesus Christ, when he conferred on his Apostles and on their successors the power to forgive sins, instituted the Sacrament of Penance in his Church, so that the faithful who had fallen into sin after their first bath of regeneration might be renewed in grace and reconciled to God.[16] For the Church "has both water and tears: the water of Baptism, the tears of Penance."[17]

II. The Reconciliation of Penitents in the Life of the Church

The Church Is Holy but, at the Same Time, Always in Need of Purification

3. Christ "loved the Church and handed himself over for her, that she might be made holy" (Eph 5:25-26), and united her to himself as a bride;[18] he fills her, who is his Body and fullness, with his divine gifts[19] and through her spreads truth and grace to all.

---

[14] *The Roman Missal*, Eucharistic Prayer III.

[15] *The Roman Missal*, Eucharistic Prayer II.

[16] Cf. Council of Trent, Session XIV, On the Sacrament of Penance, chapter 1: Denzinger-Schönmetzer 1668 and 1670; canon 1: Denzinger-Schönmetzer 1701.

[17] St. Ambrose, Letters 41, 12: *PL* 16, 1116.

[18] Cf. Rev 19:7.

[19] Cf. Eph 1:22-23; Second Vatican Council, Dogmatic Constitution on the Church, *Lumen gentium*, no. 7; *Acta Apostolicæ Sedis* 57 (1965), pp. 9-11.

The members of the Church, however, are exposed to temptation and unfortunately often fall into sin. Because of this, "while Christ, 'holy, innocent, and undefiled' (Heb 7:26), knew nothing of sin (2 Cor 5:21) but came to expiate only the sins of the people (cf. Heb 2:17), the Church, at the same time holy and always in need of being purified, embracing in her bosom sinners, always follows the way of penance and renewal."[20]

Penance in the Life and Liturgy of the Church

4. In many and various ways the People of God performs and perfects this continual repentance. For the Church, sharing in the sufferings of Christ through her own patient endurance,[21] performing works of mercy and charity,[22] conforming herself daily more and more to the Gospel of Christ, becomes a sign in the world of conversion to God. She expresses this in her life and celebrates it in her liturgy, while the faithful confess themselves to be sinners and implore the forgiveness of God and of their brothers and sisters, as happens in penitential services, in the proclamation of the word of God, in prayer, in the penitential elements of the Eucharistic Celebration.[23]

In the Sacrament of Penance the faithful truly "obtain pardon from the mercy of God for the offense

[20]Second Vatican Council, Dogmatic Constitution on the Church, *Lumen gentium*, no. 8; *ibidem*, p. 12.

[21]Cf. 1 Pt 4:13.

[22]Cf. 1 Pt 4:8.

[23]Cf. Council of Trent, Session XIV, On the Sacrament of Penance, Denzinger-Schönmetzer 1638, 1740, 1743; Sacred Congregation of Rites, Instruction *Eucharisticum mysterium*, May 25, 1967, no. 35: *Acta Apostolicæ Sedis* 59 (1967), pp. 560-561; *The Roman Missal* (2010), General Instruction, nos. 51, 52, 81, 82, and 84.

committed against him and are at the same time reconciled with the Church, which they have wounded by their sins and which by charity, example, and prayer seeks their conversion."[24]

Reconciliation with God and with the Church

5. Because sin is an offense committed against God, which disrupts our friendship with him, repentance "ultimately implies that we should love God and entrust ourselves completely to him."[25] The sinner, therefore, who by the grace of a merciful God, enters on the way of repentance, returns to the Father who "loved us first" (1 Jn 4:19), to Christ who has given himself up for us,[26] and to the Holy Spirit who has been poured out upon us in abundance.[27]

But "there reigns among people, by the hidden and benign mystery of the divine will, a supernatural solidarity whereby the sin of one harms the others just as the holiness of one also benefits the others,"[28] and so repentance always carries with it reconciliation with one's brothers and sisters, to whom sin always causes harm.

[24]Second Vatican Council, Dogmatic Constitution on the Church, *Lumen gentium*, no. 11; *Acta Apostolicæ Sedis* 57 (1965), pp. 15-16.

[25]Paul VI, Apostolic Constitution *Pænitemini*, Feb. 17, 1966: *Acta Apostolicæ Sedis* 58 (1966), p. 179; cf. Second Vatican Council, Dogmatic Constitution on the Church, *Lumen gentium*, no. 11: *Acta Apostolicæ Sedis* 57 (1965), pp. 15-16.

[26]Cf. Gal 2:20; Eph 5:25.

[27]Cf. Ti 3:6.

[28]Paul VI, Apostolic Constitution *Indulgentiarum doctrina*, Jan. 1, 1967, no. 4: *Acta Apostolicæ Sedis* 59 (1967), p. 9; cf. Pius XII, Encyclical Letter *Mystici Corporis*, June 29, 1943: *Acta Apostolicæ Sedis* 35 (1943), p. 213.

In fact, often when people commit deeds of injustice, they act together. In the same way, when they repent they help one another, so that, freed from sin by the grace of Christ, they may work together with all people of good will for justice and peace in the world.

The Sacrament of Penance and Its Parts

6. The disciple of Christ who, after sinning, is moved by the Holy Spirit and comes to the Sacrament of Penance, should, above all, turn to God with all his (her) heart. This inner conversion of heart, which involves contrition for sin and the resolution to lead a new life, is expressed by confession made to the Church, by due satisfaction (an act of penance), and also by amendment of life. God truly grants forgiveness of sins through the Church, which works by the ministry of Priests.[29]

a) *Contrition*

Among the actions of a penitent the most important is contrition, which is "heartfelt sorrow and detestation for the sin committed, with the resolve not to sin again."[30] And indeed, "we can only approach the Kingdom of Christ by 'metanoia,' that is, by an intimate change of the whole person, so that one begins to consider, to judge, and to order one's life, having been overcome by the holiness and love of God, which in these last days have been revealed in his Son and imparted to us abundantly (cf. Heb 1:2; Col 1:19 and throughout;

[29] Cf. Council of Trent, Session XIV, On the Sacrament of Penance, chapter 1: Denzinger-Schönmetzer 1673-1675.

[30] *Ibidem*, chapter 4: Denzinger-Schönmetzer 1676.

Eph 1:23 and throughout)."[31] Therefore, the genuineness of repentance depends on this contrition of heart. For conversion should affect the person from within, in order to enlighten him (her) more deeply day by day and to conform him (her) more and more to Christ.

b) *Confession*

The Sacrament of Penance involves the confession of sins, which proceeds from true knowledge of self before God and from contrition for sins. This inward examination of the heart and outward accusation, however, should be made in the light of God's mercy. Confession requires in the penitent the willingness to open his (her) heart to the minister of God; and in the minister, a spiritual judgment by which, acting in the person of Christ, he pronounces sentence for the forgiveness or retention of sins by virtue of the power of the keys.[32]

c) *Satisfaction (an Act of Penance)*

True conversion is achieved by satisfaction (an act of penance) for sins, by amendment of life, and also by reparation of injury.[33] The kind and measure of satisfaction should be suited to the individual penitent, so that each one may restore the order which he (she) has harmed and be cured by the appropriate medicine for the sickness from which he (she) has suffered. In the

---

[31] PAUL VI, Apostolic Constitution *Pænitemini*, Feb. 17, 1966: *Acta Apostolicæ Sedis* 58 (1966), p. 179.

[32] Cf. Council of Trent, Session XIV, On the Sacrament of Penance, chapter 5: Denzinger-Schönmetzer 1679.

[33] Cf. Council of Trent, Session XIV, On the Sacrament of Penance, chapter 8: Denzinger-Schönmetzer 1690-1692; PAUL VI, Apostolic Constitution *Indulgentiarum doctrina*, Jan. 1, 1967, nos. 2-3: *Acta Apostolicæ Sedis* 59 (1967), pp. 6-8.

same way, the penance should be truly a remedy for sin and in some way renew his (her) life. Thus the penitent, "forgetting those things that are past" (Phil 3:13) once again becomes part of the mystery of salvation and strains forward towards the things to come.

d) *Absolution*

Through the sign of absolution, God grants pardon to the sinner who manifests his (her) conversion to the Church's minister in sacramental confession, and thus the Sacrament of Penance is completed. For according to the design of God, in which the humanity and kindness of God our Savior have visibly appeared to people,[34] God wishes to confer salvation on us through visible signs and to renew once more the broken covenant.

Therefore, through the Sacrament of Penance the Father welcomes the son returning to him, Christ places the lost sheep on his shoulders and carries it back to the flock, and the Holy Spirit sanctifies his temple once more or inhabits it more fully. All this is manifested in a renewed and more fervent participation at the table of the Lord, at which there is great rejoicing at the banquet of the Church of God over the son returning from afar.[35]

The Necessity and Usefulness of This Sacrament

7. Just as the wound of sin is varied and manifold in the life of individuals and of the community, so too the remedy which Penance offers to us is of various kinds.

[34] Cf. Ti 3:4-5.

[35] Cf. Lk 15:7, 10, 32.

Thus, those who have fallen away by grave sin from the communion of the love of God are called back through the Sacrament of Penance to the life that they had lost. And those who fall into venial sins as a result of daily weakness receive strength through the repeated celebration of Penance, in order to attain the full freedom of the children of God.

a) To obtain the saving remedy of the Sacrament of Penance, according to the design of the merciful God, the faithful must confess to the Priest each and every grave sin which, after examining his (her) conscience, he (she) can remember.[36]

b) Moreover, the frequent and diligent use of this Sacrament is very useful, even for venial sins. For it is not a mere ritual repetition or psychological exercise, but a continuous striving to perfect the grace of Baptism, so that, as we carry in our bodies the Death of Jesus Christ, the life of Jesus may be manifested in us more and more.[37] In confessions of this kind, the penitents, as they accuse themselves of venial sins, should try, above all, to be conformed more completely to Christ and to follow more attentively the voice of the Spirit.

In order that this Sacrament of salvation may really exercise its power in Christ's faithful, it is necessary that it should take root in their whole life and move them to more fervent service of God and their brothers and sisters.

The celebration of this Sacrament is thus always an act in which the Church proclaims her faith, gives thanks

[36]Cf. Council of Trent, Session XIV, On the Sacrament of Penance, canons 7-8: Denzinger-Schönmetzer 1707-1708.

[37]Cf. 2 Cor 4:10.

to God for the freedom by which Christ has made us free,[38] and offers her life as a spiritual sacrifice in praise of the glory of God, as she hastens to meet Christ.

III. Offices and Ministries in the Reconciliation of Penitents

The Function of the Community in the Celebration of Penance

8. The whole Church, as a priestly people, acts in different ways in performing the work of reconciliation which has been entrusted to her by the Lord. For the Church not only calls sinners to repentance by preaching the word of God, but also intercedes for them and supports the penitent with maternal care and solicitude, so that he (she) may acknowledge and confess his (her) sins, and obtain mercy from God, who alone can forgive sins. Furthermore, the Church herself becomes the instrument of the conversion and absolution of the penitent, through the ministry entrusted by Christ to the Apostles and their successors.[39]

The Minister of the Sacrament of Penance

9. a) The Church exercises her ministry of the Sacrament of Penance through Bishops and Priests, who call the faithful to conversion by preaching the word of God and declare and grant the forgiveness of sins in the name of Christ and by the power of the Holy Spirit.

---

[38]Cf. Gal 4:31.

[39]Cf. Mt 18:18; Jn 20:23.

In exercising this ministry, Priests act in communion with the Bishop, who is the moderator of penitential discipline, and participate in his power and office.[40]

b) The competent minister of the Sacrament of Penance is a Priest who has the faculty of absolving in accordance with the norm of canons 967-975 of the Code of Canon Law. All Priests, however, even if not approved to hear confessions, validly and lawfully absolve any penitents without exception in danger of death.

The Pastoral Exercise of This Ministry

10. a) In order that the confessor may be able to fulfill his office correctly and faithfully, he should recognize the diseases of the soul and apply suitable remedies to them, wisely exercise the office of judge, and acquire the knowledge and prudence necessary for this task by diligent study, under the guidance of the Magisterium of the Church, especially by pouring out prayers to God. For the discernment of spirits is the intimate knowledge of the work of God in the human heart, the gift of the Holy Spirit, and the fruit of charity.[41]

b) The confessor should always be ready to hear the confessions of the faithful, whenever confession is reasonably sought by the faithful.[42]

c) The confessor exercises a paternal office when receiving a penitent sinner and leading him (her) to the light of truth, revealing the heart of the Father to people

[40]Cf. Second Vatican Council, Dogmatic Constitution on the Church, *Lumen gentium*, no. 26: *Acta Apostolicæ Sedis* 57 (1965), pp. 31-32.

[41]Cf. Phil 1:9-10.

[42]Cf. Sacred Congregation for the Doctrine of the Faith, *Pastoral Norms for the Administration of General Sacramental Absolution*, June 16, 1972, no. XII: *Acta Apostolicæ Sedis* 64 (1972), p. 514.

and displaying the image of Christ the Shepherd. He should therefore bear in mind that he has been entrusted with the ministry of Christ, who for the salvation of humanity fulfilled the work of redemption with mercy and is present by his power in the Sacraments.[43]

d) The confessor, understanding that, as the minister of God, he has come to know the secret conscience of his brother or sister, is bound by his office to keep the sacramental seal as sacrosanct.

The Penitent

11. The parts that the faithful penitent has in the Sacrament are of the greatest importance.

For, when rightly disposed, a penitent approaches this saving remedy instituted by Christ and confesses his (her) sins, he (she) by his (her) actions has a part in the Sacrament itself, which is completed by the words of absolution spoken by the minister in the name of Christ.

So the faithful, when they experience and proclaim the mercy of God in their life, celebrate together with the Priest the liturgy by which the Church constantly renews herself.

IV. The Celebration of the Sacrament of Penance

The Place of Celebration

12. The Sacrament of Penance is usually celebrated, unless a just cause intervenes, in a church or oratory.

[43]Cf. Second Vatican Council, Constitution on the Sacred Liturgy, *Sacrosanctum Concilium*, no. 7: *Acta Apostolicæ Sedis* 56 (1964), pp. 100-101.

The Conference of Bishops is to establish norms regarding the confessional; it is to take care, however, that there are always confessionals with a fixed grate between the penitent and the confessor in an open place so that the faithful who wish to can use them freely.

Confessions are not to be heard outside a confessional without a just cause.[43A]

The Time of Celebration

13. The reconciliation of penitents can be celebrated at any time and on any day. It is desirable, however, that the faithful should know the day and time at which a Priest is present to exercise this ministry. The faithful should be encouraged to approach the Sacrament of Penance at a time when Mass is not being celebrated, especially during the scheduled times.[44]

The season of Lent is most suitable for the celebration of the Sacrament of Penance, because already on Ash Wednesday the solemn invitation resounds before the People of God: "Repent and believe in the Gospel." It is therefore fitting that several penitential celebrations should be held during Lent, so that the

[43A]Cf. *Code of Canon Law*, canon 964; United States Conference of Catholic Bishops, complementary norm to the *Code of Canon Law*, canon 964, §2 (2000): "Provision must be made in each church or oratory for a sufficient number of places for sacramental confessions which are clearly visible, truly accessible, and which provide a fixed grille between the penitent and the confessor. Provision should also be made for penitents who wish to confess face-to-face, with due regard for the Authentic Interpretation of canon 964, §2 by the Pontifical Council for the Interpretation of Legislative Texts, July 7, 1998 (*AAS* 90 [1998], 711)."

[44]Cf. Sacred Congregation of Rites, Instruction *Eucharisticum mysterium*, May 25, 1967, no. 35; *Acta Apostolicæ Sedis* 59 (1967), pp. 560-561.

opportunity may be offered to all the faithful to be reconciled with God and their brothers and sisters and to celebrate with hearts renewed the Paschal Mystery in the Most Sacred Triduum.

Liturgical Vestments

14. The norms laid down by the local Ordinaries, regarding the liturgical vestments for the celebration of Penance, should be observed.

A. The Order for Reconciling Individual Penitents

The Preparation of the Priest and the Penitent

15. Priest and penitent should first prepare themselves by prayer to celebrate the Sacrament. The Priest should call upon the Holy Spirit, that he may receive light and charity from the Spirit; the penitent, on the other hand, should compare his (her) life with the example and commandments of Christ and pray to God for the forgiveness of his (her) sins.

The Reception of the Penitent

16. The Priest should receive the penitent with fraternal charity, and, if there is need, greet him (her) with friendly words. Then the penitent signs himself (herself) with the Sign of the Cross, saying: In the name of the Father, and of the Son, and of the Holy Spirit. Amen. The Priest may also do this with the penitent. Then the Priest, in a few words, invites the penitent to trust in God. If the penitent is unknown to the confessor, it is appropriate for the penitent to indicate his (her) state

in life, also the time of his (her) last confession, his (her) difficulties in leading the Christian life, and other things which it is useful for the confessor to know in exercising his ministry.

THE READING OF THE WORD OF GOD

17. Then, if appropriate, the Priest, or the penitent himself (herself), reads some text from Sacred Scripture, or this may be done in preparation for the celebration of the Sacrament. For through the word of God each of the faithful is enlightened to recognize his (her) sins and is called to conversion and to trust in the mercy of God.

THE CONFESSION OF SINS AND THE ACCEPTANCE OF SATISFACTION (AN ACT OF PENANCE)

18. The penitent then confesses his (her) sins, beginning, where it is the custom, with the formula of general confession I confess to almighty God. The Priest, if there is need, may help the penitent to make an integral confession and, moreover, encourage him (her) to repent sincerely for offenses committed against God. Finally the Priest should offer the penitent suitable counsels for beginning a new life, and, if necessary, instruct him (her) in the duties of the Christian life.

If, however, the penitent has been the cause of harm or scandal, the Priest should lead him (her) to resolve to make suitable reparation.

Then the Priest imposes satisfaction (an act of penance) on the penitent. This should not only make up for the past, but also be a help towards a new life and a remedy for weakness, and thus, as far as possible, should correspond to the gravity and nature of the sins.

Satisfaction (an act of penance) may suitably be performed by prayer, by self-denial, and especially by service of one's neighbor and by works of mercy, which illustrate that sin and its forgiveness have a social aspect.

The Prayer of the Penitent and the Absolution by the Priest

19. After this the penitent manifests his (her) contrition and resolution to lead a new life through some prayer in which the forgiveness of God the Father is implored. It is desirable that the prayer should be based upon words of Sacred Scripture.

Then, after the prayer of the penitent, the Priest, extending his hands, or at least his right hand, over the head of the penitent, pronounces the formula of absolution in which the essential words are: I absolve you from your sins, in the name of the Father, and of the Son, and of the Holy Spirit. When he says these last words, the Priest makes the Sign of the Cross over the penitent. The words of absolution (cf. no. 46, p. 45) indicate that the reconciliation of the penitent proceeds from the mercy of the Father; it shows the connection between the reconciliation of the sinner and the Paschal Mystery of Christ; it stresses the role of the Holy Spirit in the forgiveness of sins; finally it sheds light on the ecclesial aspect of the Sacrament, because reconciliation with God is sought and given through the ministry of the Church.

The Proclamation of Praise and the Dismissal of the Penitent

20. Having received forgiveness for his (her) sins, the penitent proclaims the mercy of God and gives thanks

to God in a short invocation taken from Sacred Scripture; then the Priest dismisses the penitent in peace.

The penitent then continues his (her) conversion and expresses it in a life transformed according to the Gospel of Christ and steeped more and more in the love of God, for "love covers a multitude of sins" (1 Pt 4:8).

The Shorter Rite

21. When pastoral need dictates, the Priest may omit or shorten some parts of the rite, but must always preserve in their entirety: the confession of sins and the acceptance of satisfaction (an act of penance), the invitation to contrition (no. 44), the formula of absolution, and the words of dismissal. If, however, there is imminent danger of death, it suffices that the Priest say the essential words of the formula of absolution, namely: I ABSOLVE YOU FROM YOUR SINS, IN THE NAME OF THE FATHER, AND OF THE SON, AND OF THE HOLY SPIRIT.

B. The Order for Reconciling Several Penitents with Individual Confession and Absolution

22. When several penitents are gathered together to receive sacramental reconciliation, it is fitting that they should be prepared for it by a celebration of the word of God.

Nevertheless, others of the faithful who will approach the Sacrament at another time, may also take part in the same celebration.

A common celebration more clearly manifests the ecclesial nature of Penance. For the faithful together hear the word of God, which proclaims the mercy of God and invites them to conversion. At the same time, they examine the conformity of their lives to the same word of God and assist each other by their mutual prayers. After each one has confessed his (her) sins and received absolution, all praise God together for his wonderful works accomplished for the good of the people whom he has gained for himself by the Blood of his Son.

If necessary, several Priests should be present, in suitable places, to be able to hear confessions individually and reconcile the faithful.

The Introductory Rites

23. When the faithful are gathered, if appropriate, a suitable liturgical song is sung. Then the Priest greets the faithful and he himself, or another minister, if necessary, briefly introduces them to the celebration and instructs them about the order of the service. Then he invites all to pray and, after brief silence, completes the prayer.

The Celebration of the Word of God

24. The Sacrament of Penance should begin with the hearing of the word, because through his word God calls people to penance and leads them to a true conversion of heart.

One or more readings may be chosen. If there is more than one, a Psalm, another suitable liturgical song, or a period of silence may be placed between them, so that the word of God may be understood more deeply and the assent of the heart may be given to it. If there is only one reading, it is desirable that it should be taken from the Gospel.

Readings should be chosen in which, in a special way:

a) the voice of God calls people to conversion and to an ever-greater conformity with Christ;

b) the mystery of reconciliation, through the Death and Resurrection of Christ and through the gift of the Holy Spirit, is placed before the eyes of those present;

c) the judgment of God about good and evil in the lives of people is recounted, to aid awareness and assist in the examination of conscience.

25. A homily, taking its starting point from the text of Scripture, should lead the penitents to an examination of conscience, to a turning away from sins, and to a turning toward God. It should remind the faithful that sin acts against God, against the community and neighbor, and against the sinner himself (herself). Therefore it would be well to recall:

a) the infinite mercy of God, which is greater than all our sins and by which God himself calls us back, again and again, to himself;

b) the need for interior repentance, by which we are also sincerely disposed to make reparation for harm caused by sin;

c) the social aspect of grace and sin, by which the actions of individuals in some way affect the whole Body of the Church;

d) the duty to make satisfaction for sin, which receives its strength from the satisfaction of Christ and requires especially, besides the works of penance, the exercise of true charity toward God and neighbor.

26. After the Homily, a suitable period of silence should be allowed for an examination of conscience to take

place and for arousing a true contrition for sins. The Priest himself or a Deacon or another minister may help the faithful with brief statements or a litany, adapted to their condition, age, etc.

If it seems appropriate, this communal examination of conscience and arousing of contrition may substitute for the Homily; but in this case, it should clearly take as its starting point the text of Sacred Scripture read earlier.

The Rite of Reconciliation

27. Then at the invitation of the Deacon or another minister, all kneel or bow and say a formula of general confession (e.g., I confess to almighty God). Afterwards, they stand and, if appropriate, recite a litany or sing a suitable liturgical song, in which they express confession of sins, contrition of heart, petition for forgiveness, and trust in the mercy of God. The Lord's Prayer is never omitted and is said at the end.

28. After the Lord's Prayer has been said, the Priests go to the places designated for hearing confessions. The penitents who desire to confess their sins go to the Priest of their choice and, after receiving appropriate satisfaction (an act of penance), are absolved by him with the formula for reconciling an individual penitent.

29. When the confessions have been completed, the Priests return to the sanctuary. The Priest who is presiding over the celebration invites all to offer thanks, by which the faithful confess the mercy of God. This may be done by a Psalm or hymn, or even by a litany. Finally the Priest concludes the celebration with a prayer, praising God for the great love with which God has loved us.

The Dismissal of the People

30. When the thanksgiving has been completed, the Priest blesses the faithful. Then the Deacon, or the Priest himself, dismisses the assembly.

C. The Order for Reconciling Penitents with General Confession and Absolution

The Discipline of General Absolution

31. Individual and integral confession and absolution constitute the only ordinary means by which a member of the faithful conscious of grave sin is reconciled with God and the Church. Only physical or moral impossibility excuses from confession of this type; in such a case reconciliation can be obtained by other means.

Absolution cannot be imparted in a general manner to many penitents at once without previous individual confession unless:

a) danger of death is imminent and there is insufficient time for the Priest or Priests to hear the confessions of the individual penitents;

b) there is grave necessity, that is, when in view of the number of penitents, there are not enough confessors available to hear the confessions of individuals properly within a suitable period of time in such a way that the penitents are forced to be deprived for a long while of sacramental grace or Holy Communion through no fault of their own. Sufficient necessity is not considered to exist when confessors cannot be present due only to the large number of penitents such as can occur on some great feast or pilgrimage.[45]

---

[45]Cf. *Code of Canon Law*, canons 960 and 961, §1.

32. It belongs to the Diocesan Bishop to judge whether the conditions given above in no. 31 are present. He can determine the cases of such necessity, attentive to the criteria agreed upon with the other members of the Conference of Bishops.[46]

33. For a member of the Christian faithful validly to receive sacramental absolution given to many at one time, it is required not only that the person is properly disposed but also at the same time intends to confess within a suitable period of time each grave sin which at the present time cannot be so confessed.

Insofar as it can be done even on the occasion of the reception of general absolution, the Christian faithful are to be instructed about the requirements mentioned above. An exhortation that each person take care to make an act of contrition is to precede general absolution even in the case of danger of death, if there is time.[47]

34. Those who have been forgiven grave sins by general absolution should go to individual confession as soon as they have the opportunity, before another reception of general absolution, unless they are impeded by just cause. Nevertheless, unless some moral impossibility prevents it, they are absolutely bound to go to confession within a year. For they are also bound by the precept, that all the faithful must individually confess

[46]Cf. *Code of Canon Law,* canon 961, §2; the United States Conference of Catholic Bishops' complementary norm to the *Code of Canon Law,* canon 961, §1, 2° (1989), "interprets the meaning of *diu* of canon 961, §1, 2° to be 'one month,' by which the Diocesan Bishop judges whether and when the conditions of grave necessity for general absolution are verified in his diocese."

[47]Cf. *Code of Canon Law,* canon 962, §§1 and 2.

to a Priest, at least once a year, each and every grave sin that has not already been confessed.[48]

The Rite of General Absolution

35. For reconciling penitents with general confession and absolution in the cases prescribed by law, everything is done as described above for a celebration for reconciling several penitents with individual confession and absolution, with the following changes only.

a) After the Homily, or in the Homily itself, the faithful who wish to take advantage of general absolution are to be reminded that they should be properly disposed, that is, each one should repent of each of his (her) transgressions and resolve to abstain from these sins, intend to make reparation for any scandal or harm he (she) may have caused, and also resolve to confess individually at the proper time each of the grave sins that cannot now be confessed.[49] In addition, some act of satisfaction to be performed should be proposed to all, to which each individual may add something, if he (she) desires.

b) Then a Deacon or other minister or the Priest himself invites the penitents who wish to receive absolution to indicate this by some kind of sign (e.g., by bowing the head, or by kneeling, or by some other sign determined by the Conferences of Bishops). The penitents together say a formula of general confession (e.g., I confess to almighty God), after which a litany or

---

[48]Cf. Sacred Congregation for the Doctrine of the Faith, *Pastoral Norms for the Administration of General Sacramental Absolution*, June 16, 1972, nos. VII and VIII: *Acta Apostolicæ Sedis* 64 (1972), pp. 512-513; *Code of Canon Law*, canons 963, 989.

[49]Cf. *ibidem*, no. VI, p. 512.

penitential song may take place. The Lord's Prayer is then said or sung by all together, as is stated above, no. 27.

c) Then the Priest says the invocation through which the grace of the Holy Spirit is sought for the forgiveness of sins, the victory over sin by the Death and Resurrection of Christ is proclaimed, and sacramental absolution is given to the penitents.

d) Finally the Priest invites all to offer thanks, as is said above, no. 29, and omitting the concluding prayer, immediately blesses the people and dismisses them.

V. Penitential Celebrations

Nature and Structure

36. Penitential celebrations are gatherings of the People of God to hear the word of God, which invites them to conversion and to renewal of life as well as announces our freedom from sin through the Death and Resurrection of Christ. Their structure is that which is usually followed in celebrations of the word of God[50] and which is set out in the Order for Reconciling Several Penitents.

It is appropriate, therefore, that after the Introductory Rites (liturgical song, greeting, and prayer) one or more readings from Sacred Scripture be read, interspersed with liturgical songs or Psalms or periods of silence. Through the Homily, these readings should be explained and applied to the assembled faithful. Nothing prohibits including, either before or after the readings from Scripture, other readings from the Fathers or other writers that would help the community and each individual

[50]Cf. Sacred Congregation of Rites, Instruction *Inter Œcumenici*, Sept. 26, 1964, nos. 37-39: *Acta Apostolicæ Sedis* 56 (1964), pp. 110-111.

attain a true awareness of sin and true contrition of heart, in other words, help bring about conversion.

After the Homily and meditation on the word of God, it is desirable that the gathering of the faithful should pray with one heart and one voice, through some litany or in another way suitable for promoting the participation of the faithful. Finally, the Lord's Prayer should always be said, so that God our Father may "forgive us our trespasses as we forgive those who trespass against us and . . . deliver us from evil." The Priest, or the minister who presides over the gathering, concludes with a prayer and the dismissal of the people.

Usefulness and Importance

37. Care should be taken that, in the minds of the faithful, these celebrations not be confused with the celebration of the Sacrament of Penance itself.[51] Nevertheless, these penitential celebrations are very useful for promoting conversion and purification of heart.[52]

Penitential celebrations may be appropriately arranged especially:

—to foster the spirit of penance in the Christian community;

—to help the faithful to prepare for confession, which may be made individually later, at a convenient time;

—to instruct children gradually to form their conscience about sin in human life and about freedom from sin through Christ;

—to help catechumens during their conversion.

[51]Cf. Sacred Congregation for the Doctrine of the Faith, *Pastoral Norms for the Administration of General Sacramental Absolution,* June 16, 1972, no. X: *Acta Apostolicæ Sedis* 64 (1972), pp. 513-514.

[52]*Ibidem.*

Moreover, where there is no Priest available to confer sacramental absolution, penitential celebrations are very useful, since they offer help towards perfect contrition, which comes from charity, by which the faithful may pursue the grace of God through a desire for sacramental Penance in the future.[53]

VI. Adaptations of the Rite to Various Regions and Circumstances

Adaptations that the Conferences of Bishops May Make

38. It is for the Conferences of Bishops, in preparing particular Rituals, to adapt this *Order of Penance* to the needs of the particular regions, so that, once their decisions have been accorded the *confirmatio* or *recognitio* of the Apostolic See, they may be used in the regions to which they pertain. In this regard, it is for the Conferences of Bishops:

a) to establish norms for the discipline of the Sacrament of Penance, especially those affecting the ministry of Priests, once their decisions have been accorded the *recognitio* of the Apostolic See;

b) to determine more precisely norms about the confessional for the ordinary celebration of the Sacrament of Penance (cf. above, no. 12) and about the signs of penitence to be made by the faithful during General Absolution (cf. above, no. 35), once their decisions have been accorded the *recognitio* of the Apostolic See;

[53]Cf. Council of Trent, Session XIV, On the Sacrament of Penance, chapter 5: Denzinger-Schönmetzer 1677.

c) to prepare versions of texts, truly accommodated to the character and language of each people, and also to approve them, once their decisions have been accorded the *confirmatio* of the Apostolic See. They may also compose new texts for the prayers of the faithful or of the minister, but preserving intact the sacramental formula, once their decisions have been accorded the *recognitio* of the Apostolic See.

Things Pertaining to the Bishop

39. It belongs to the Diocesan Bishop:

a) to regulate the discipline of Penance in his own diocese,[54] including appropriate adaptations to the rite according to the norms proposed by the Conference of Bishops;

b) to determine the cases of necessity in which it is permitted to confer sacramental absolution in a general manner, attentive to the conditions established by law (cf. above, no. 31) and the criteria agreed upon with the other members of the Conference of Bishops.[55]

Adaptations within the Competence of the Minister

40. It pertains to Priests, especially pastors:

a) in the celebration of reconciliation, whether for individuals or for the community, to adapt the rite to

[54]Cf. Second Vatican Council, Dogmatic Constitution on the Church, *Lumen gentium*, no. 26: *Acta Apostolicæ Sedis* 57 (1965), pp. 31-32.

[55]Cf. Sacred Congregation for the Doctrine of the Faith, *Pastoral Norms for the Administration of General Sacramental Absolution*, June 16, 1972, no. V: *Acta Apostolicæ Sedis* 64 (1972), p. 512; *Code of Canon Law* canon 961, §§1 and 2.

the concrete circumstances of the penitents, keeping intact the essential structure and the formula of absolution. They may leave out certain parts of it, if necessary for pastoral reasons, or may add others that will be more enriching, may select the texts of the readings or the prayers, may choose a place better suited to the celebration, according to the norms laid down by the Conference of Bishops, so that the whole celebration may be enriching and fruitful;

b) to schedule and prepare penitential celebrations at various times during the year, especially during Lent. They may be assisted by others, including the laity, so that the texts chosen and the order of celebration may be truly accommodated to the condition and circumstances of the community or group (e.g., children, the sick, etc.).

1

CHAPTER I

THE ORDER FOR RECONCILING INDIVIDUAL PENITENTS

THE ORDER FOR RECONCILING INDIVIDUAL PENITENTS

1

The Reception of the Penitent

41. When the penitent comes to confess his (her) sins, the Priest welcomes him (her) with kindness and greets him (her) with friendly words.

42. Then the penitent and, if appropriate, the Priest as well, sign themselves with the Sign of the Cross, saying:

In the name of the Father, and of the Son,
and of the Holy Spirit. Amen.

The Priest invites the penitent to have trust in God, in these or similar words:

May God, who has shone his light
in our hearts
grant that you may truly know your sins
and his mercy.

The penitent replies:

Amen.

Other optional texts, nos. 67-71.

The Reading of the Word of God (Optional)

43. Then, if appropriate, the Priest reads or recites from memory a text of Sacred Scripture in which God's mercy is announced and people are called to conversion.

The texts are found at nos. 72-84.

The Confession of Sins and the Acceptance of Satisfaction

44. Next, the penitent confesses his (her) sins, after first saying, where it is the custom, a general formula for confession (e.g., I confess to almighty God).

If necessary, the Priest assists the penitent to make an integral confession, offers him (her) suitable counsel, and urges him (her) to have contrition for his (her) faults, reminding him (her) that through the Sacrament of Penance a Christian, by dying and rising with Christ, is renewed in the Paschal Mystery. Then the Priest proposes a work of penance that the penitent accepts to make satisfaction for sin and to amend his (her) life.

The Priest should take care that he adapts to the penitent's circumstances in every way, whether in the manner of speaking or even in the counsel provided.

The Prayer of the Penitent and the Absolution

45. The Priest then invites the penitent to express his (her) contrition, which the penitent may do in these or similar words:

O my God,
I am sorry and repent with all my heart
for all the wrong I have done
and for the good I have failed to do,
because by sinning I have offended you,
who are all good and worthy
    to be loved above all things.
I firmly resolve,
    with the help of your grace,
to do penance,
to sin no more,
and to avoid the occasions of sin.
Through the merits of the Passion
    of our Savior Jesus Christ,
Lord, have mercy.

Other optional texts, nos. 85-92.

46. Then the Priest, extending his hands over the penitent's head (or at least extending his right hand), says:

God, the Father of mercies,
through the Death and Resurrection
    of his Son
has reconciled the world to himself
and poured out the Holy Spirit
    for the forgiveness of sins;
through the ministry of the Church
may God grant you pardon and peace.
AND I ABSOLVE YOU FROM YOUR SINS,
IN THE NAME OF THE FATHER, AND OF THE SON, ✠
    AND OF THE HOLY SPIRIT.

The penitent replies:

Amen.

The Proclamation of Praise of God and the Dismissal of the Penitent

47. After the absolution, the Priest continues:

Give thanks to the Lord for he is good.

The penitent concludes:

For his mercy endures for ever.

Then the Priest dismisses the penitent who has been reconciled, saying:

The Lord has forgiven your sins.
Go in peace.

Other optional texts, no. 93.

2

CHAPTER II

THE ORDER FOR RECONCILING SEVERAL PENITENTS WITH INDIVIDUAL CONFESSION AND ABSOLUTION

THE ORDER FOR RECONCILING SEVERAL PENITENTS WITH INDIVIDUAL CONFESSION AND ABSOLUTION

THE INTRODUCTORY RITES

LITURGICAL SONG

48. When the faithful are gathered, and as the Priest enters the church, if appropriate, a Psalm, antiphon, or other appropriate liturgical song may be sung, e.g.:

Answer us, Lord, for your mercy is kind;
in the abundance of your mercies,
look upon us.

Or:

With boldness let us approach
the throne of grace,
that we may receive mercy
and find grace as a timely help.

GREETING

49. When the singing is concluded the Priest begins with the Sign of the Cross, then greets those present:

Grace, mercy, and peace to you
from God the Father
and Christ Jesus our Savior.

℟. And with your spirit.

Or:

Grace and peace to you
from God the Father and from Jesus Christ,
who loved us and washed away our sins
in his Blood.

℟. To him be glory for ever and ever. Amen.

Other optional texts, nos. 94-96.

Then the Priest himself or another minister instructs those present with a brief address about the importance and purpose of the celebration and about the order of the service.

Prayer

50. Then the Priest invites all to pray, in these or similar words:

Let us pray, brothers and sisters (brethren),
that God, who calls us to conversion,
will grant us the grace
of true and fruitful repentance.

And all pray in silence for a while. Then the Priest says the prayer:

Graciously hear the prayers
of those who call upon you,
we ask, O Lord,
and forgive the sins of those
who confess to you,
granting us in your kindness
both pardon and peace.
Through Christ our Lord.

All:

Amen.

Or:

Set your Spirit in our midst, O Lord,
to wash us in the cleansing waters
of repentance
and to make of us a living sacrifice to you,
so that, as he gives us life,
we may everywhere praise your glory
and confess your mercy.
Through Christ our Lord.

All:

Amen.

Other optional texts, nos. 97-100.

The Celebration of the Word of God

51. Then the celebration of the word begins. If there are several readings, a Psalm or other appropriate liturgical song or even a period of silence should intervene between them, so that the word of God may be understood more deeply by everyone and heartfelt assent be given to it. If there is only one reading, it is desirable that it be taken from the Gospel.

FIRST EXAMPLE

"Love is the fullness of the law"

FIRST READING Deuteronomy 5:1-3, 6-7, 11-12, 16-21a; 6:4-6

Love the Lord your God with all your heart.

A reading from the Book of Deuteronomy

Moses summoned all Israel and said to them,
"Hear, O Israel, the statutes and decrees
which I proclaim in your hearing this day,
that you may learn them and take care to observe them.
The LORD, our God, made a covenant with us at Horeb;
not with our fathers did the LORD make this covenant,
but with us, all of us who are alive here this day."

He said:
" 'I, the LORD, am your God,
who brought you out of the land of Egypt,
that place of slavery.
You shall not have other gods beside me.

'You shall not take the name of the LORD, your God, in vain.
For the LORD will not leave unpunished
him who takes his name in vain.

'Take care to keep holy the sabbath day
as the LORD, your God, commanded you.

'Honor your father and your mother,
as the LORD, your God, has commanded you,
that you may have a long life and prosperity in the land
which the LORD, your God, is giving you.

'You shall not kill.

'You shall not commit adultery.

'You shall not steal.

'You shall not bear dishonest witness against your neighbor.

'You shall not covet your neighbor's wife.

'You shall not desire your neighbor's house or field.' "

"Hear, O Israel!
The LORD is our God, the LORD alone!
Therefore, you shall love the LORD, your God,
with all your heart, and with all your being,
and with your whole strength.
Take to heart these words which I enjoin on you today."

The word of the Lord.

RESPONSORIAL PSALM Baruch 1:15-18a, 18b-19, 20, 21-22

℟. (3:2) Hear, O Lord, and have mercy, for you are a merciful God.

Justice is with the LORD, our God;
and we today are flushed with shame,
we men of Judah and citizens of Jerusalem,
that we, with our kings and rulers and priests and prophets, and with our fathers,
have sinned in the LORD's sight and disobeyed him.—℟.

We have neither heeded the voice of the LORD, our God,
nor followed the precepts which the LORD set before us.
From the time the LORD led our fathers out of the land of Egypt
until the present day,
we have been disobedient to the LORD, our God,
and only too ready to disregard his voice.—℟.

And the evils and the curse which the LORD enjoined upon Moses, his servant,
at the time he led our fathers forth from the land of Egypt
to give us the land flowing with milk and honey,
cling to us even today.—℟.

For we did not heed the voice of the LORD, our God,
in all the words of the prophets whom he sent us,

but each one of us went off after the devices of our own wicked hearts,
served other gods, and did evil in the sight of the LORD, our God.—℟.

SECOND READING Ephesians 5:1-14

Live in love, as Christ loved us.

A reading from the Letter of Saint Paul to the Ephesians

Be imitators of God, as beloved children, and live in love,
as Christ loved us and handed himself over for us
as a sacrificial offering to God for a fragrant aroma.
Immorality or any impurity or greed
must not even be mentioned among you,
as is fitting among holy ones,
no obscenity or silly or suggestive talk, which is out of place,
but instead, thanksgiving.
Be sure of this,
that no immoral or impure or greedy person, that is, an idolater,
has any inheritance in the Kingdom of Christ and of God.
Let no one deceive you with empty arguments,
for because of these things
the wrath of God is coming upon the disobedient.

So do not be associated with them.
For you were once darkness,
but now you are light in the Lord.
Live as children of light,
for light produces every kind of goodness and righteousness and truth.
Try to learn what is pleasing to the Lord.
Take no part in the fruitless works of darkness;
rather expose them,
for it is shameful even to mention the things done by them in secret;
but everything exposed by the light becomes visible,
for everything that becomes visible is light.
Therefore, it says:
"Awake, O sleeper,
and arise from the dead,
and Christ will give you light."

The word of the Lord.

GOSPEL ACCLAMATION John 8:12

I am the light of the world, says the Lord;
whoever follows me will have the light of life.

GOSPEL

Matthew 22:34-40

The whole law and the prophets depend on these two commandments.

✠ A reading from the holy Gospel
according to Matthew

When the Pharisees heard that Jesus had silenced the Sadducees,
they gathered together, and one of them,
a scholar of the law, tested him by asking,
"Teacher, which commandment in the law is the greatest?"

He said to him,
"You shall love the Lord, your God, with all your heart,
with all your soul, and with all your mind.
This is the greatest and the first commandment.
The second is like it:
You shall love your neighbor as yourself.
The whole law and the prophets depend on these two commandments."

The Gospel of the Lord.

Or:

2 John 13:34-35; 15:10-13

I give you a new commandment.

✠ A reading from the holy Gospel
according to John

Jesus said to his Apostles:
"I give you a new commandment: love one another.

As I have loved you, so you also should love one another.
This is how all will know that you are my disciples,
if you have love for one another."

"If you keep my commandments, you will remain in my love,
just as I have kept my Father's commandments
and remain in his love.

"I have told you this so that my joy may be in you
and your joy may be complete.
This is my commandment: love one another as I love you.
No one has greater love than this,
to lay down one's life for one's friends."

The Gospel of the Lord.

SECOND EXAMPLE

"Your mind must be renewed"

FIRST READING Isaiah 1:10-18

Cease doing evil; learn to do good.

A reading from the
Book of the Prophet Isaiah

Hear the word of the LORD,
princes of Sodom!

Listen to the instruction of our God,
people of Gomorrah!
What care I for the number of your sacrifices?
says the LORD.
I have had enough of whole-burnt rams
and fat of fatlings;
In the blood of calves, lambs and goats
I find no pleasure.

When you come in to visit me,
who asks these things of you?
Trample my courts no more!
Bring no more worthless offerings;
your incense is loathsome to me.
New moon and sabbath, calling of assemblies,
octaves with wickedness: these I cannot bear.
Your new moons and festivals I detest;
they weigh me down, I tire of the load.
When you spread out your hands,
I close my eyes to you;
Though you pray the more,
I will not listen.
Your hands are full of blood!
Wash yourselves clean!
Put away your misdeeds from before my eyes;
cease doing evil; learn to do good.
Make justice your aim: redress the wronged,
hear the orphan's plea, defend the widow.

Come now, let us set things right,
says the LORD:
Though your sins be like scarlet,
they may become white as snow;
Though they be crimson red,
they may become white as wool.

The word of the Lord.

RESPONSORIAL PSALM Psalm 51 (50):3-4, 5-6, 7-9, 10-11, 12-13, 14-15, 16-17, 18-19, 20-21

Instead of the entire Psalm, a selection of stanzas which form a coherent whole may be chosen, but in this case the stanza marked with an asterisk (vv. 18-19) should be included.

℟. (19a) My sacrifice to God is a broken spirit.

Have mercy on me, O God,
according to your merciful love;
according to your great compassion,
blot out my transgressions.
Wash me completely from my iniquity,
and cleanse me from my sin.—℟.

My transgressions, truly I know them;
my sin is always before me.
Against you, you alone, have I sinned;
what is evil in your sight I have done.
So you are just in your sentence,
without reproach in your judgment.—℟.

Behold, in guilt I was born,
a sinner when my mother conceived me.

Behold, you delight in sincerity of heart;
in secret you teach me wisdom.
Cleanse me with hyssop, and I shall be pure;
wash me, and I shall be whiter than snow.—℟.

Let me hear rejoicing and gladness,
that the bones you have crushed may exult.
Turn away your face from my sins,
and blot out all my guilt.—℟.

Create a pure heart for me, O God;
renew a steadfast spirit within me.
Do not cast me away from your presence;
take not your holy spirit from me.—℟.

Restore in me the joy of your salvation;
sustain in me a willing spirit.
I will teach transgressors your ways,
that sinners may return to you.—℟.

Rescue me from bloodshed, O God,
O God of my salvation,
and then my tongue shall ring out your justice.
O Lord, open my lips
and my mouth shall proclaim your praise.—℟.

*For in sacrifice you take no delight;
burnt offering from me would not please you.

My sacrifice to God, a broken spirit:
a broken and humbled heart,
you will not spurn, O God.—℟.

In your good pleasure, show favor to Zion;
rebuild the walls of Jerusalem.
Then you will delight in right sacrifice,
burnt offerings wholly consumed.
Then you will be offered young bulls on your altar.—℟.

SECOND READING

Ephesians 4:23-32

Be renewed in the spirit of your minds.

A reading from the Letter of
Saint Paul to the Ephesians

Brothers and sisters:
Be renewed in the spirit of your minds,
and put on the new self,
created in God's way in righteousness and holiness of truth.
Therefore, putting away falsehood,
speak the truth,
each one to his neighbor,
for we are members one of another.
Be angry but do not sin;
do not let the sun set on your anger,
and do not leave room for the Devil.
The thief must no longer steal,
but rather labor,
doing honest work with his own hands,
so that he may have something to share with one in need.

No foul language should come out of your mouths,
but only such as is good for needed edification,
that it may impart grace to those who hear.
And do not grieve the Holy Spirit of God,
with which you were sealed for the day of redemption.
All bitterness, fury, anger, shouting, and reviling
must be removed from you,
along with all malice.
And be kind to one another, compassionate,
forgiving one another as God has forgiven you in Christ.

The word of the Lord.

Gospel Acclamation — Matthew 11:28

Come to me, all you that labor and are burdened,
and I will give you rest, says the Lord.

Gospel — Matthew 5:1-12

Blessed are the poor in spirit.

✠ A reading from the holy Gospel according to Matthew

When Jesus saw the crowds, he went up the mountain,
and after he had sat down, his disciples came to him.

He began to teach them, saying:

"Blessed are the poor in spirit,
for theirs is the Kingdom of heaven.
Blessed are they who mourn,
for they will be comforted.
Blessed are the meek,
for they will inherit the land.
Blessed are they who hunger and thirst for righteousness,
for they will be satisfied.
Blessed are the merciful,
for they will be shown mercy.
Blessed are the clean of heart,
for they will see God.
Blessed are the peacemakers,
for they will be called children of God.
Blessed are they who are persecuted for the sake of righteousness,
for theirs is the Kingdom of heaven.
Blessed are you when they insult you and persecute you
and utter every kind of evil against you falsely because of me.
Rejoice and be glad,
for your reward will be great in heaven.
Thus they persecuted the prophets who were before you."

The Gospel of the Lord.

Other optional texts, nos. 101-201.

Homily

52. The Homily follows which, taking its starting point from the text of the readings, should lead the penitents to examine their consciences and renew their lives.

Examination of Conscience

53. It is appropriate for a period of silence to be observed in order to complete an examination of conscience and to awaken a true contrition for sin. The Priest, Deacon, or another minister may assist the faithful by brief statements or some form of litany, taking into consideration their circumstances, age, etc.

The Rite of Reconciliation

General Confession of Sins

54. At the invitation of a Deacon, or of another minister, all kneel or bow, and together say a general formula for confession (e.g., I confess to almighty God). Then they stand and, if appropriate, use a litany or an appropriate liturgical song. The Lord's Prayer is never omitted and is added at the end.

First Example

Deacon or minister:

Brothers and sisters (Brethren),
confess your sins,
and pray for one another
that you may be saved.

All recite together:

I confess to almighty God
and to you, my brothers and sisters,
that I have greatly sinned,
in my thoughts and in my words,
in what I have done
and in what I have failed to do,

And, striking their breast, they say:

through my fault, through my fault,
through my most grievous fault;

Then they continue:

therefore I ask blessed Mary, ever-Virgin,
all the Angels and Saints,
and you, my brothers and sisters,
to pray for me to the Lord our God.

Deacon or minister:

**Let us humbly beseech the Lord of mercies,
to grant forgiveness to the guilty
and healing to the wounded,
for he purifies the hearts
of those who confess
and frees from every bond of iniquity
those who accuse themselves.**

**—That you will grant us
the grace of true repentance.**

℟. Lord, we ask you, hear our prayer.

**—That you may pardon your servants
and graciously ease the debt
of their past offenses.**

℟. Lord, we ask you, hear our prayer.

**—That your children,
who have strayed from
the holiness of the Church by sinning,
may obtain pardon for the sins they confess
and be restored to her unharmed.**

℟. Lord, we ask you, hear our prayer.

**—That those whose Baptism
has been sullied by the stain of sin
may be restored to their former splendor.**

℟. Lord, we ask you, hear our prayer.

**—That, readmitted to your sacred altars,
they may be transformed by the hope
of eternal glory.**

℟. Lord, we ask you, hear our prayer.

**—That, with sincere devotion,
they may henceforth remain faithful
to your Sacraments
and always hold fast to you as Lord.**

℟. Lord, we ask you, hear our prayer.

**—That, renewed by your charity,
they may become witnesses in the world
to your love.**

℟. Lord, we ask you, hear our prayer.

—That they may faithfully persevere
in keeping your commandments
and come to possess life without end.

℟. Lord, we ask you, hear our prayer.

Deacon or minister:

Let us now ask God our Father
to forgive us our trespasses
and deliver us from all evil,
as we pray to him in the words
Christ has taught us:

All say together:

Our Father, who art in heaven,
hallowed be thy name;
thy kingdom come,
thy will be done
on earth as it is in heaven.
Give us this day our daily bread,
and forgive us our trespasses,
as we forgive those who trespass against us;
and lead us not into temptation,
but deliver us from evil.

The Priest concludes:

Draw near to your servants, O Lord,
so that those who confess in your Church
that they are sinners
may be freed through her from every sin
and, with hearts renewed,
be worthy to give you thanks.
Through Christ our Lord.

All:

Amen.

SECOND EXAMPLE

Deacon or minister:

Brothers and sisters (Brethren),
calling to mind the kindness
of God our Father,
let us confess our sins,
that we may obtain his mercy.

All recite together:

I confess to almighty God
and to you, my brothers and sisters,
that I have greatly sinned,
in my thoughts and in my words,
in what I have done
and in what I have failed to do,

And, striking their breast, they say:

through my fault, through my fault,
through my most grievous fault;

Then they continue:

therefore I ask blessed Mary, ever-Virgin,
all the Angels and Saints,
and you, my brothers and sisters,
to pray for me to the Lord our God.

Deacon or minister:

**Let us humbly pray to Christ our Savior,
whom we have as a righteous advocate
with the Father,
that he will forgive us our sins
and cleanse us from all iniquity.**

**—You were sent to bring good news
to the poor
and to heal the contrite of heart.**

℟. Lord, be merciful to me, a sinner.

Or:

℟. Lord, have mercy.

**—You did not come to call the righteous,
but sinners.**

℟. Lord, be merciful to me, a sinner.

Or:

℟. Lord, have mercy.

**—You forgave much
to the woman who loved much.**

℟. Lord, be merciful to me, a sinner.

Or:

℟. Lord, have mercy.

**—You did not refuse to sit at table
with tax collectors and sinners.**

℟. Lord, be merciful to me, a sinner.

Or:

℟. Lord, have mercy.

**—You carried the lost sheep
on your shoulders back to the fold.**

℟. Lord, be merciful to me, a sinner.

Or:

℟. Lord, have mercy.

—You did not condemn the woman
taken in adultery
but told her to go in peace.

℟. Lord, be merciful to me, a sinner.

Or:

℟. Lord, have mercy.

—You called Zacchaeus the tax collector
to conversion and new life.

℟. Lord, be merciful to me, a sinner.

Or:

℟. Lord, have mercy.

—You promised paradise
to the repentant thief.

℟. Lord, be merciful to me, a sinner.

Or:

℟. Lord, have mercy.

—You are seated at the right hand
of the Father,
and live for ever to intercede for us.

℟. Lord, be merciful to me, a sinner.

Or:

℟. Lord, have mercy.

Deacon or minister:

Let us now pray together to the Father
as Christ himself commanded us,
that, as we forgive one another
our trespasses,
he will forgive us our sins:

All say together:

Our Father, who art in heaven,
hallowed be thy name;
thy kingdom come,
thy will be done
on earth as it is in heaven.
Give us this day our daily bread,
and forgive us our trespasses,
as we forgive those who trespass against us;
and lead us not into temptation,
but deliver us from evil.

The Priest concludes:

O God, who have prepared helps
suited to our weakness,
grant, we pray,
that we may receive their healing effects
with joy
and reflect them in a holy way of life.
Through Christ our Lord.

All:

Amen.

Other optional texts, nos. 202-205.

Individual Confession and Absolution

55. Then the penitents go to the Priests stationed in suitable locations and confess their sins to them, and, after receiving and accepting appropriate satisfaction (an act of penance), they are absolved by them individually. After hearing the confession and, if appropriate,

offering suitable counsel, the Priest, omitting everything else that is customary in reconciling an individual penitent and extending his hands over the penitent's head (or at least extends his right hand), imparts the absolution, saying:

God, the Father of mercies,
through the Death and Resurrection
of his Son
has reconciled the world to himself
and poured out the Holy Spirit
for the forgiveness of sins;
through the ministry of the Church
may God grant you pardon and peace.
AND I ABSOLVE YOU FROM YOUR SINS,
IN THE NAME OF THE FATHER, AND OF THE SON, ✠
AND OF THE HOLY SPIRIT.

The penitent replies:

Amen.

PROCLAMATION OF PRAISE FOR GOD'S MERCY

56. When the individual confessions have been completed, the Priest who is presiding over the celebration, with the other Priests near him, invites all present to offer thanks and encourages them to do good works by which the grace of repentance in the life of each one and of the entire community will be shown. It is therefore appropriate for all to sing a Psalm or hymn or to say a litany to acknowledge God's power and mercy, for example, the Canticle of the Blessed Virgin Mary or Psalm 136 (135):1-9, 13-14, 16, 24-26.

Luke 1:46-55
Canticle of Mary (*Magnificat*)

46 My soul proclaims the greatness of the Lord
47 and my spirit rejoices in God my Savior,
48 for he has looked upon his handmaid in her lowliness;
for behold, from this day forward
all generations will call me blessed.

49 For the Almighty has done great things for me,
and holy is his name.
50 His mercy is from age to age
for those who fear him.

51 He has made known the strength of his arm,
and has scattered the proud in their conceit of heart.
52 He has cast down the mighty from their thrones
and has exalted those who are lowly.
53 He has filled the hungry with good things,
and has sent the rich away empty.

54 He has helped his servant Israel,
mindful of his mercy
55 even as he promised to our fathers,
to Abraham and his descendants forever.

Psalm 136 (135):1-9, 13-14, 16, 24-26

1 O give thanks to the LORD, for he is good,
for his mercy endures forever.

2 Give thanks to the God of gods,
for his mercy endures forever.
3 Give thanks to the Lord of lords,
for his mercy endures forever;

4 who alone has wrought marvelous works,
for his mercy endures forever;
5 who in wisdom made the heavens,
for his mercy endures forever;
6 who spread the earth on the waters,
for his mercy endures forever;

7 It was he who made the great lights,
for his mercy endures forever;
8 the sun to rule in the day,
for his mercy endures forever;
9 the moon and the stars in the night,
for his mercy endures forever;

13 The Red Sea he divided in two,
for his mercy endures forever;
14 he made Israel pass through the midst,
for his mercy endures forever;
16 through the desert his people he led,
for his mercy endures forever;

24 And he snatched us away from our foes,
for his mercy endures forever;
25 He gives bread to all mortal flesh,
for his mercy endures forever;
26 To the God of heaven give thanks,
for his mercy endures forever.

Other optional texts, no. 206.

Concluding Prayer of Thanksgiving

57. After the song of praise or the litany, the Priest concludes the common prayer:

**Almighty and merciful God,
who wonderfully created human nature,
and still more wonderfully restored it,
you do not abandon sinners,
but pursue them with a father's love;
you sent your Son into the world
to destroy sin and death by his Passion
and restore life and joy to us
by the Resurrection;
you poured the Holy Spirit into our hearts
that we might be your children and heirs;
you constantly renew us
by the Sacraments of salvation,
that we may be freed from slavery to sin
and be transformed more fully day by day
into the image of your beloved Son.**

**We give you thanks
for the wonders of your mercy
and praise you with the whole Church,
singing to you a new song
with voice, heart, and deed.
To you be glory, through Christ,
in the Holy Spirit,
now and for ever.**

All:

Amen.

Or:

**Holy Father,
who have restored us
in the image of your Son,
grant, we pray, that, having obtained mercy,
we may become a sign
of your love in the world.
Through Christ our Lord.**

All:

Amen.

Other optional texts, nos. 207-211.

The Concluding Rites

58. The Priest says:

The Lord be with you.

All:

And with your spirit.

A Deacon may say the invitation:

Bow down for the blessing.

Then the Priest blesses all present:

**May the Lord guide your hearts
in the love of God
and the patience of Christ.**

All:

Amen.

May you walk in newness of life
and please God in all things.

All:

Amen.

And may almighty God bless you,
the Father, and the Son, ✠
and the Holy Spirit.

All:

Amen.

Other optional texts, nos. 212-214.

59. Then a Deacon, or other minister or the Priest himself, dismisses the assembly:

The Lord has forgiven your sins.
Go in peace.

All:

Thanks be to God.

Or another appropriate formula.

3

CHAPTER III

THE ORDER FOR RECONCILING SEVERAL PENITENTS WITH GENERAL CONFESSION AND ABSOLUTION

THE ORDER FOR RECONCILING SEVERAL PENITENTS WITH GENERAL CONFESSION AND ABSOLUTION

60. For reconciling several penitents with general confession and absolution, in the cases provided for in the law, everything is done as described above for a celebration for reconciling several penitents with individual confession and absolution, with the following changes only. 3

INSTRUCTION

After the Homily, or in the Homily itself, the faithful who wish to receive general absolution should be instructed that they should be properly disposed, that is, each one should repent of his (her) transgressions and resolve to abstain from these sins, to intend to make reparation for any scandal and harm he (she) may have caused, and also to resolve to confess individually at the proper time each of the grave sins that cannot now be confessed. In addition, some satisfaction (an act of penance) to be performed should be proposed to all, to which each individual may add something if he (she) desires.

GENERAL CONFESSION

61. Then a Deacon or other minister or the Priest himself invites the penitents who wish to receive absolution to indicate this by some kind of sign. For example:

Let those who now wish to receive
sacramental absolution
kneel and make the general confession.

Or:

Let those who now wish to receive
sacramental absolution
bow down and make the general confession.

The penitents say a formula for general confession (e.g., I confess to almighty God), after which, a litany or appropriate liturgical song may occur, as described above for reconciling several penitents with individual confession and absolution (no. 54). At the end, the Lord's Prayer is always added.

General Absolution

62. The Priest then imparts the absolution, saying, with hands extended over the penitents:

May God the Father,
who does not desire the death of sinners
but rather that they turn back and live,
and who first loved us
and sent his Son into the world,
so that the world might be saved
through him,
show you his mercy
and give you peace.

℟. Amen.

**May the Lord Jesus Christ,
who was handed over for our transgressions
and rose again for our justification
and who poured the Holy Spirit
upon his Apostles,
so that they might receive the power
to forgive sins,
now, through our ministry,
free you from evil
and fill you with the Holy Spirit.**

℟. Amen.

**May the Holy Spirit, the Paraclete,
who was given to us
for the forgiveness of sins
and in whom we have access to the Father,
purify your hearts and make you radiant
with his splendor,
so that you may proclaim
the mighty works of him
who called you out of darkness
into his marvelous light.**

℟. Amen.

AND I ABSOLVE YOU FROM YOUR SINS,
IN THE NAME OF THE FATHER, AND OF THE SON, ✠
AND OF THE HOLY SPIRIT.

℟. Amen.

Or:

God, the Father of mercies,
through the Death and Resurrection
of his Son
has reconciled the world to himself
and poured out the Holy Spirit
for the forgiveness of sins;
through the ministry of the Church
may God grant you pardon and peace.
AND I ABSOLVE YOU FROM YOUR SINS,
IN THE NAME OF THE FATHER, AND OF THE SON, ✠
AND OF THE HOLY SPIRIT.

℟. Amen.

PROCLAMATION OF PRAISE AND CONCLUSION

63. The Priest then invites all to offer thanks and to acknowledge God's mercy. After a suitable liturgical song or hymn, omitting the concluding prayer, he immediately blesses the people and dismisses them, as indicated in the Order for Reconciling Several Penitents with Individual Confession and Absolution, nos. 58-59.

SHORTER RITE

64. In case of urgent necessity, the Order for Reconciling Several Penitents with General Confession and Absolution may be shortened. After a brief reading from Sacred Scripture, if appropriate, and after giving the usual instruction (no. 60) and proposing satisfaction (an act of penance), the penitents are immediately invited to make a general confession (e.g., I confess to almighty God), and the Priest imparts absolution to them with the invocation indicated above in no. 62.

65. However, in imminent danger of death, it is enough for the Priest to use the formula of absolution alone, which in this case may be shortened thus:

AND I ABSOLVE YOU FROM YOUR SINS,
IN THE NAME OF THE FATHER, AND OF THE SON, ✠
AND OF THE HOLY SPIRIT.

℟. Amen.

66. Those faithful who have been absolved from grave sins through general sacramental absolution, are bound to confess such grave sins individually at their next individual confession.

CHAPTER IV

VARIOUS TEXTS TO BE USED IN THE CELEBRATION OF RECONCILIATION

A Ω

VARIOUS TEXTS TO BE USED IN THE CELEBRATION OF RECONCILIATION

I. For the Reconciliation of One Penitent

Invitation to Trust in God

67. (Ezekiel 33:11)

Come with trust to the Lord,
who does not wish the sinner to die
but to turn back to him and live.

VT

68. (Luke 5:32)

May the Lord Jesus welcome you.
He came to call sinners, not the just.
Have confidence in him.

69.

May the grace of the Holy Spirit
illumine your heart,
so that with confidence
you may confess your sins
and come to know the mercy of God.

70.

May the Lord be in your heart,
that you may confess your sins
with a contrite spirit.

71. (1 John 2:1-2)

If you have sinned, do not lose heart.
We have an advocate with the Father,
Jesus Christ the Righteous One:
he is the atonement for our sins,
and not for our sins only
but for those of the whole world.

Short Readings from Sacred Scripture

72. Isaiah 53:4-6

Let us look to Jesus,
who suffered for our salvation and rose again for our justification.

It was our infirmities that he bore,
our sufferings that he endured,
While we thought of him as stricken,
as one smitten by God and afflicted.
But he was pierced for our offenses,
crushed for our sins;
Upon him was the chastisement that makes us whole,
by his stripes we were healed.
We had all gone astray like sheep,
each following his own way;
But the Lord laid upon him
the guilt of us all.

73. Ezekiel 11:19-20

Let us listen to the Lord as he speaks to us:

I will give them a new heart
and put a new spirit within them;
I will remove the stony heart from their bodies,
and replace it with a natural heart,
so that they will live according to my statutes,
and observe and carry out my ordinances;
thus they shall be my people and I will be their God.

74. Matthew 6:14-15

Let us listen to the Lord as he speaks to us:

"If you forgive men their transgressions,
your heavenly Father will forgive you.
But if you do not forgive men,
neither will your Father forgive your transgressions."

75. Mark 1:14-15

After John had been arrested,
Jesus came to Galilee proclaiming the Gospel of God:
"This is the time of fulfillment.
The Kingdom of God is at hand.
Repent, and believe in the Gospel."

76. Luke 6:31-38

Let us listen to the Lord as he speaks to us:

"Do to others as you would have them do to you.

For if you love those who love you,
what credit is that to you?
Even sinners love those who love them.
And if you do good to those who do good to you,
what credit is that to you?
Even sinners do the same.
If you lend money to those from whom you expect repayment,
what credit is that to you?
Even sinners lend to sinners,
and get back the same amount.
But rather, love your enemies and do good to them,
and lend expecting nothing back;
then your reward will be great
and you will be children of the Most High,
for he himself is kind to the ungrateful and the wicked.
Be merciful, just as also your Father is merciful.

"Stop judging and you will not be judged.
Stop condemning and you will not be condemned.
Forgive and you will be forgiven.
Give and gifts will be given to you;
a good measure, packed together, shaken down, and overflowing,
will be poured into your lap.
For the measure with which you measure
will in return be measured out to you."

77. Luke 15:1-7

Tax collectors and sinners were all drawing near to listen to Jesus,
but the Pharisees and scribes began to complain, saying,
"This man welcomes sinners and eats with them."
So to them Jesus addressed this parable.
"What man among you having a hundred sheep and losing one of them
would not leave the ninety-nine in the desert
and go after the lost one until he finds it?
And when he does find it,
he sets it on his shoulders with great joy
and, upon his arrival home,
he calls together his friends and neighbors and says to them,
'Rejoice with me because I have found my lost sheep.'
I tell you, in just the same way
there will be more joy in heaven over one sinner who repents
than over ninety-nine righteous people
who have no need of repentance."

78. John 20:19-23

On the evening of that first day of the week,
when the doors were locked, where the disciples were,
for fear of the Jews,

Jesus came and stood in their midst
and said to them, "Peace be with you."
When he had said this, he showed them his hands and his side.
The disciples rejoiced when they saw the Lord.
Jesus said to them again, "Peace be with you.
As the Father has sent me, so I send you."
And when he had said this, he breathed on them and said to them,
"Receive the Holy Spirit.
Whose sins you forgive are forgiven them,
and whose sins you retain are retained."

79. Romans 5:8-9

God proves his love for us
in that while we were still sinners Christ died for us.
How much more then, since we are now justified by his Blood,
will we be saved through him from the wrath.

80. Ephesians 5:1-2

So be imitators of God, as beloved children, and live in love,
as Christ loved us and handed himself over for us
as a sacrificial offering to God for a fragrant aroma.

81. Colossians 1:12-14

Let us give thanks to the Father who has made us worthy
to share the heritage of the holy ones in light.
He delivered us from the power of darkness
and transferred us to the kingdom of his beloved Son,
in whom we have redemption, the forgiveness of sins.

82. Colossians 3:8-10, 12-17

Now you must put them all away:
anger, fury, malice, slander,
and obscene language out of your mouths.
Put to death, then, the parts of you that are earthly:
immorality, impurity, passion, evil desire,
and the greed that is idolatry.
Stop lying to one another,
since you have taken off the old self with its practices
and have put on the new self,
which is being renewed, for knowledge,
in the image of its creator.

Put on, as God's chosen ones, holy and beloved,
heartfelt compassion, kindness, humility, gentleness, and patience,
bearing with one another and forgiving one another,

if one has a grievance against another;
as the Lord has forgiven you, so must you also do.
And over all these put on love,
that is, the bond of perfection.
And let the peace of Christ control your hearts,
the peace into which you were also called in one Body.
And be thankful.
Let the word of Christ dwell in you richly,
as in all wisdom you teach and admonish one another,
singing psalms, hymns, and spiritual songs
with gratitude in your hearts to God.
And whatever you do, in word or in deed,
do everything in the name of the Lord Jesus,
giving thanks to God the Father through him.

83. 1 John 1:6-7, 9

If we say, "We have fellowship with him,"
while we continue to walk in darkness,
we lie and do not act in truth.
But if we walk in the light as he is in the light,
then we have fellowship with one another,
and the Blood of his Son Jesus cleanses us from all sin.
If we acknowledge our sins, he is faithful and just

and will forgive our sins and cleanse us
from every wrongdoing.

84. A reading may also be chosen from those proposed below in nos. 101-201 for the reconciliation of several penitents. Likewise, the Priest and penitent may optionally use other readings from Sacred Scripture.

Prayer of the Penitent

85. (Psalm 25 [24]:6-7)

Remember, Lord, the compassion
and mercy you showed long ago.
Do not recall my sins and failings.
In your mercy remember me, Lord,
because of your goodness.

86. (Psalm 51 [50]:4-5)

Wash me, O Lord, from my iniquity
and cleanse me from my sin.
I acknowledge my offense;
my sin is before me always.

87. (Luke 15:18; 18:13)

Father, I have sinned against you
and I am not worthy to be called your son.
Be merciful to me, a sinner.

88.

O God, most merciful Father,
like the Prodigal Son,
I turn to you and say:
I have sinned against you;
I am no longer worthy
to be called your child.

O Jesus Christ, Savior of the world,
like the thief to whom
    you opened the gates of paradise,
    I beg you:
Lord, remember me in your Kingdom.

O Holy Spirit, fount of love,
with trust I call upon you:
Purify me;
make me walk as a child of the light.

89.

Lord Jesus,
who opened the eyes of the blind,
    healed the sick,
forgave the sinful woman,
and, after his denial,
    confirmed Peter in your love,
hear my plea:
forgive all my sins,
renew me in your love,
and grant that I may live
    in perfect communion
with my brothers and sisters
and so proclaim your salvation to all.

90.

Lord Jesus,
who chose to be called
    the friend of sinners,
through the mystery of your Death
    and Resurrection,
free me from my sins.

May your peace grow strong in me,
that I may bear the fruits
of charity, justice, and truth.

91.

Lord Jesus Christ, Lamb of God,
who take away the sin of the world,
through the grace of the Holy Spirit
be pleased to reconcile me
with your Father;
cleanse me in your Blood from every fault
and make me fully alive
to the praise of your glory.

92.

Have mercy on me, O God,
according to your merciful love;
turn your face from my sins
and blot out all my guilt;
create a pure heart in me, O God,
renew an upright spirit deep within me.

Or:

Lord Jesus, Son of God,
have mercy on me, a sinner.

Or:

O my God,
I am heartily sorry
for having offended you,
and I detest all my sins
because of your just punishments,
but most of all because they offend you,
my God,

who are all good and deserving
of all my love.
I firmly resolve,
with the help of your grace,
to sin no more
and to avoid the near occasions of sin.
Amen.

AFTER THE ABSOLUTION

93. In place of the proclamation of God's praise and the formula of dismissal, the Priest may say:

May the Passion of our Lord Jesus Christ,
the intercession of the Blessed Virgin Mary
and of all the Saints,
whatever good you do
and whatever evil you endure,
be for you a remedy for sin,
an increase of grace,
and the reward of eternal life.
Go in peace.

Or:

The Lord has freed you from sin.
May he grant you salvation
in his heavenly Kingdom.
To him be glory for ever.

℟. Amen.

Or:

Blessed are they whose iniquity is forgiven
and whose sin is blotted out.

Be glad, brother (sister),
and rejoice in the Lord.
Go in peace.

Or:

Go in peace,
and proclaim to the world
the marvelous works of God,
who has saved you.

II. For the Reconciliation of Several Penitents

Texts for the Greeting

94.

Grace, mercy, and peace to you
from God the Father
and from Jesus Christ, the Son of the Father,
in truth and in love.

℟. Amen.

95.

Brothers and sisters (Brethren),
may God open your heart
to his law and give you peace;
may he hear your prayers
and be reconciled with you.

℟. Amen.

96.

Grace to you and peace
from God our Father
and from the Lord Jesus Christ,
who gave himself up for our sins.

℟. To him be glory for ever and ever. Amen.

Likewise, the greetings proposed for the beginning of Mass may be used.

Prayers over the People Gathered Together

97.

In your mercy, we pray, O Lord,
absolve us from all sin,
so that when we receive pardon
for our offenses,
we may serve you in freedom of heart.
Through Christ our Lord.

℟. Amen.

98.

O Lord our God,
who are not thwarted by our offenses,
but are moved to forgiveness
by our works of penance,
look, we pray, on us your servants,
who confess to you that we have sinned.
Grant that we may celebrate
the Sacraments of your mercy

and, with our conduct amended,
may delight in the everlasting joys
you bestow on us.
Through Christ our Lord.

℟. Amen.

99.

Almighty and merciful God,
in the name of your Son
you have gathered us into one,
that we may receive mercy
and find grace as a timely help.
Open our eyes to see the wrong
we have done
and touch our hearts
that we may turn to you in truth.

May your love restore to unity
those whom sin has divided and scattered.
May your power heal and strengthen
those wounded through frailty.
May your Spirit bring to new life
those whom death has held captive.
So, with charity restored in us,
may the image of your Son
shine forth in our works,
and, with his glory resplendent
on the face of the Church,
may all people know
that you have sent him,
Jesus Christ, your Son, our Lord.

℟. Amen.

100.

Father of mercies
and God of all consolation,
who have said that you desire
not the death of sinners
but their conversion,
come to the aid of your people,
that they may return to you and live.
Help us, so that, as we hear your words,
we may confess our sins
and give thanks to you
for the forgiveness we have received,
and, as we live the truth in charity,
we may, through all things,
grow in Christ your Son,
who lives and reigns for ever and ever.

℟. Amen.

Biblical Readings

The readings proposed here have been selected for the benefit of pastors and the faithful. For diversity, and according to the special nature of the assembly, other readings may be chosen.

Readings from the Old Testament

Genesis 3:1-19 .... page 107
Genesis 4:1-15 .... page 109
Genesis 18:17-33 .... page 111
Exodus 17:1-7 .... page 113
Exodus 20:1-21 .... page 114
Deuteronomy 6:4-9 .... page 116
Deuteronomy 9:7-19 .... page 117
Deuteronomy 30:15-20 .... page 119
2 Samuel 12:1-9, 13 .... page 120
Nehemiah 9:1-20 .... page 122
Wisdom 1:1-16 .... page 125
Wisdom 5:1-16 .... page 127
Sirach 28:1-7 .... page 128
Isaiah 1:2-6, 15-18 .... page 129
Isaiah 5:1-7 .... page 130
Isaiah 43:22-28 .... page 131
Isaiah 53:1-12 .... page 132
Isaiah 55:1-11 .... page 134
Isaiah 58:1-11 .... page 135
Isaiah 59:1-4, 9-15 .... page 137
Jeremiah 2:1-13 .... page 139
Jeremiah 7:21-26 .... page 140
Ezekiel 11:14-21 .... page 141
Ezekiel 18:20-32 .... page 142
Ezekiel 36:23-28 .... page 144
Hosea 2:16-25 .... page 145
Hosea 11:1-11 .... page 146
Hosea 14:2-10 .... page 148
Joel 2:12-19 .... page 149
Micah 6:1-15 .... page 150
Micah 7:2-7, 18-20 .... page 152
Zechariah 1:1-6 .... page 153

Responsorial Psalms

Psalm 13 (12):2-3, 4-5, 6 .... page 154
Psalm 25 (24):1b-3, 4-5, 6, 7, 8-9, 10-11, 12-14, 15-16, 17-18, 19-20, 21-22 .... page 155
Psalm 31 (30):2-3a, 3b-4, 5-6 .... page 156
Psalm 32 (31):1-2, 3-4, 5, 6, 7, 8, 9, 10, 11 .... page 157
Psalm 36 (35):2, 3-4, 5, 6-7, 8, 9-10, 11-13 .... page 158
Psalm 50 (49):7, 8 and 14-15, 16-17, 18-19, 20-21, 22-23 .... page 159
Psalm 51 (50):3-4, 5-6, 7-9, 10-11, 12-13, 14-15, 16-17, 18-19, 20-21 .... page 160
Psalm 73 (72):1-3, 4-5, 6-7, 8-9, 10-12, 13-15, 16-17, 18-20, 21-22, 23-24, 25-26, 27-28 .... page 161
Psalm 90 (89):1-2, 3-4, 5-6, 7-8, 9-10, 11-12, 13-15, 16-17 .... page 163
Psalm 95 (94):1-2, 3-5, 6-7b, 7c-9, 10-11 .... page 164
Psalm 119 (118):1 and 10-11, 12-13, 15-16 .... page 165
Psalm 123 (122):1, 2, 3-4 .... page 166
Psalm 130 (129):1-2, 3-4, 5-6b, 6c-8 .... page 166
Psalm 139 (138):1-3, 4-6, 7-8, 9-10, 11-12, 13-14, 15, 16, 17-18, 23-24 .... page 167
Psalm 143 (142):1-2, 3-4, 5-6, 7, 8, 9-10, 11 .... page 168

Readings from the New Testament

Romans 3:22-26 .... page 170
Romans 5:6-11 .... page 170
Romans 6:2-13 .... page 171
Romans 6:16-23 .... page 173
Romans 7:14-25 .... page 174
Romans 12:1-2, 9-19 .... page 175
Romans 13:8-14 .... page 176
2 Corinthians 5:17-21 .... page 177
Galatians 5:16-24 .... page 178
Ephesians 2:1-10 .... page 179
Ephesians 4:1-3, 17-32 .... page 180
Ephesians 5:1-14 .... page 182
Ephesians 6:10-18 .... page 183
Colossians 3:1-10, 12-17 .... page 184
Hebrews 12:1-5 .... page 186
James 1:22-27 .... page 186
James 2:14-26 .... page 187
James 3:1-12 .... page 189
1 Peter 1:13-23 .... page 190
2 Peter 1:3-11 .... page 191
1 John 1:5—2:2 .... page 192
1 John 2:3-11 .... page 193
1 John 3:1-24 .... page 194
1 John 4:16-21 .... page 197
Revelation 2:1-5 .... page 197
Revelation 3:14-22 .... page 198
Revelation 20:11-15 .... page 199
Revelation 21:1-8 .... page 200

Gospel Readings

Matthew 3:1-12 .... page 201
Matthew 4:12-17 .... page 203
Matthew 5:1-12 .... page 203
Matthew 5:13-16 .... page 204
Matthew 5:17-47 .... page 205
Matthew 9:1-8 .... page 208
Matthew 9:9-13 .... page 209
Matthew 18:15-20 .... page 210
Matthew 18:21-35 .... page 211
Matthew 25:31-46 .... page 212
Matthew 26:69-75 .... page 214
Mark 12:28-34 .... page 215
Luke 7:36-50 .... page 216
Luke 13:1-5 .... page 217
Luke 15:1-10 .... page 218
Luke 15:11-32 .... page 219
Luke 17:1-4 .... page 222
Luke 18:9-14 .... page 222
Luke 19:1-10 .... page 223
Luke 23:39-43 .... page 224
John 8:1-11 .... page 225
John 8:31-36 .... page 226
John 15:1-8 .... page 227
John 15:9-14 .... page 228
John 19:13-37 .... page 228
John 20:19-23 .... page 231

Readings from the Old Testament

101.

Gn 3:1-19

She took some of its fruit and ate it.

A reading from the Book of Genesis

Now the serpent was the most cunning of all the animals
that the LORD God had made.
The serpent asked the woman,
"Did God really tell you not to eat
from any of the trees in the garden?"
The woman answered the serpent:
"We may eat of the fruit of the trees in the garden;
it is only about the fruit of the tree
in the middle of the garden that God said,
'You shall not eat it or even touch it, lest you die.' "
But the serpent said to the woman:
"You certainly will not die!
No, God knows well that the moment you eat of it
your eyes will be opened and you will be like gods
who know what is good and what is evil."
The woman saw that the tree was good for food,
pleasing to the eyes, and desirable for gaining wisdom.
So she took some of its fruit and ate it;
and she also gave some to her husband, who was with her,
and he ate it.
Then the eyes of both of them were opened,
and they realized that they were naked;
so they sewed fig leaves together
and made loincloths for themselves.

When they heard the sound of the LORD God moving about in the garden
at the breezy time of the day,
the man and his wife hid themselves from the LORD God
among the trees of the garden.
The LORD God called to Adam and asked him, "Where are you?"
He answered, "I heard you in the garden;
but I was afraid, because I was naked,
so I hid myself."
Then he asked, "Who told you that you were naked?
You have eaten, then,
from the tree of which I had forbidden you to eat!"
The man replied, "The woman whom you put here with me—
she gave me fruit from the tree, and so I ate it."
The LORD God then asked the woman,
"Why did you do such a thing?"
The woman answered, "The serpent tricked me into it, so I ate it."

Then the LORD God said to the serpent:

"Because you have done this, you shall be banned from all the animals
and from all the wild creatures;
On your belly shall you crawl,
and dirt shall you eat
all the days of your life.
I will put enmity between you and the woman,
and between your offspring and hers;
He will strike at your head,
while you strike at his heel."

To the woman he said:

"I will intensify the pangs of your childbearing;
in pain shall you bring forth children.
Yet your urge shall be for your husband,
and he shall be your master."

To the man he said: "Because you listened to your wife
and ate from the tree of which I had forbidden you to eat,

"Cursed be the ground because of you!
In toil shall you eat its yield
all the days of your life.
Thorns and thistles shall it bring forth to you,
as you eat of the plants of the field.
By the sweat of your face
shall you get bread to eat,
Until you return to the ground,
from which you were taken;
For you are dirt,
and to dirt you shall return."

The word of the Lord.

VT

---

102. Gn 4:1-15

Cain attacked his brother Abel and killed him.

A reading from the Book of Genesis

The man had relations with his wife Eve,
and she conceived and bore Cain, saying,
"I have produced a man with the help of the LORD."
Next she bore his brother Abel.
Abel became a keeper of flocks, and Cain a tiller of the soil.
In the course of time Cain brought an offering to the LORD

from the fruit of the soil,
while Abel, for his part,
brought one of the best firstlings of his flock.
The LORD looked with favor on Abel and his offering,
but on Cain and his offering he did not.
Cain greatly resented this and was crestfallen.
So the LORD said to Cain:
"Why are you so resentful and crestfallen?
If you do well, you can hold up your head;
but if not, sin is a demon lurking at the door:
his urge is toward you, yet you can be his master."

Cain said to his brother Abel, "Let us go out in the field."
When they were in the field,
Cain attacked his brother Abel and killed him.
Then the LORD asked Cain, "Where is your brother Abel?"
He answered, "I do not know.
Am I my brother's keeper?"
The LORD then said: "What have you done!
Listen: your brother's blood cries out to me from the soil!
Therefore you shall be banned from the soil
that opened its mouth to receive
your brother's blood from your hand.
If you till the soil, it shall no longer give you its produce.
You shall become a restless wanderer on the earth."
Cain said to the LORD: "My punishment is too great to bear.
Since you have now banished me from the soil,
and I must avoid your presence
and become a restless wanderer on the earth,
anyone may kill me at sight."

"Not so!" the LORD said to him.
"If anyone kills Cain, Cain shall be avenged sevenfold."
So the LORD put a mark on Cain, lest anyone should kill him at sight.

The word of the Lord.

---

103. Gn 18:17-33

For the sake of those ten, I will not destroy it.

A reading from the Book of Genesis

The LORD reflected: "Shall I hide from Abraham what I am about to do,
now that he is to become a great and populous nation,
and all the nations of the earth are to find blessing in him?
Indeed, I have singled him out
that he may direct his children and his household after him
to keep the way of the LORD
by doing what is right and just,
so that the LORD may carry into effect for Abraham
the promises he made about him."
Then the LORD said:
"The outcry against Sodom and Gomorrah is so great,
and their sin so grave,
that I must go down and see whether or not their actions
fully correspond to the cry against them that comes to me.
I mean to find out."

While the two men walked on farther toward Sodom,
the LORD remained standing before Abraham.
Then Abraham drew nearer to him and said:
"Will you sweep away the innocent with the guilty?
Suppose there were fifty innocent people in the city;
would you wipe out the place, rather than spare it
for the sake of the fifty innocent people within it?
Far be it from you to do such a thing,
to make the innocent die with the guilty,
so that the innocent and the guilty would be treated alike!
Should not the judge of all the world act with justice?"
The LORD replied,
"If I find fifty innocent people in the city of Sodom,
I will spare the whole place for their sake."
Abraham spoke up again:
"See how I am presuming to speak to my Lord,
though I am but dust and ashes!
What if there are five less than fifty innocent people?
Will you destroy the whole city because of those five?"
He answered, "I will not destroy it if I find forty-five there."
But Abraham persisted, saying, "What if only forty are found there?"
He replied, "I will forbear doing it for the sake of forty."
Then Abraham said, "Let not my Lord grow impatient if I go on.
What if only thirty are found there?"

He replied, "I will forbear doing it if I can find but thirty there."
Still Abraham went on,
"Since I have thus dared to speak to my Lord, what if there are no more than twenty?"
He answered, "I will not destroy it for the sake of the twenty."
But he still persisted:
"Please, let not my Lord grow angry if I speak up this last time.
What if there are at least ten there?"
He replied, "For the sake of those ten, I will not destroy it."

The LORD departed as soon as he had finished speaking with Abraham,
and Abraham returned home.

The word of the Lord.

---

104. Ex 17:1-7

They tested the LORD, saying,
"Is the LORD in our midst or not?"

A reading from the Book of Exodus

From the desert of Sin the whole congregation of the children of Israel
journeyed by stages, as the LORD directed,
and encamped at Rephidim.

There was no water for the people to drink.
They quarreled, therefore, with Moses and said,
"Give us water to drink."
Moses replied, "Why do you quarrel with me?
Why do you put the LORD to a test?"
[...] Then, in their thirst for water,
the people grumbled against Moses,
saying, "Why did you ever make us leave Egypt?

Was it just to have us die here of thirst
with our children and our livestock?"
So Moses cried out to the LORD,
"What shall I do with this people?
A little more and they will stone me!"
The LORD answered Moses,
"Go over there in front of the people,
along with some of the elders of Israel,
holding in your hand, as you go,
the staff with which you struck the river.
I will be standing there in front of you on the rock in Horeb.
Strike the rock, and the water will flow from it
for the people to drink."
This Moses did, in the presence of the elders of Israel.
The place was called Massah and Meribah,
because the children of Israel quarreled there
and tested the LORD, saying,
"Is the LORD in our midst or not?"

The word of the Lord.

---

105. Ex 20:1-21

I, the LORD, am your God.
You shall not have other gods.

A reading from the Book of Exodus

God delivered all these commandments:

"I, the LORD, am your God,
who brought you out of the land of Egypt, that place of slavery.
You shall not have other gods besides me.
You shall not carve idols for yourselves
in the shape of anything in the sky above

or on the earth below or in the waters beneath the earth;
you shall not bow down before them or worship them.
For I, the LORD, your God, am a jealous God,
inflicting punishment for their fathers' wickedness
on the children of those who hate me,
down to the third and fourth generation;
but bestowing mercy down to the thousandth generation
on the children of those who love me and keep my commandments.

VT

"You shall not take the name of the LORD, your God, in vain.
For the LORD will not leave unpunished
him who takes his name in vain.

"Remember to keep holy the sabbath day.
Six days you may labor and do all your work,
but the seventh day is the sabbath of the LORD, your God.
No work may be done then either by you, or your son or daughter,
or your male or female slave, or your beast,
or by the alien who lives with you.
In six days the LORD made the heavens and the earth,
the sea and all that is in them;
but on the seventh day he rested.
That is why the LORD has blessed the sabbath day and made it holy.

"Honor your father and your mother,
that you may have a long life in the land
which the LORD, your God, is giving you.

"You shall not kill.

"You shall not commit adultery.

"You shall not steal.

"You shall not bear false witness against your neighbor.

"You shall not covet your neighbor's house.
You shall not covet your neighbor's wife,
nor his male or female slave, nor his ox or ass
nor anything else that belongs to him."

When the people witnessed the thunder and lightning,
the trumpet blast and the mountain smoking,
they all feared and trembled.
So they took up a position much farther away
and said to Moses,
"You speak to us, and we will listen;
but let not God speak to us, or we shall die."
Moses answered the people,
"Do not be afraid,
for God has come to you only to test you and put his fear upon you,
lest you should sin."
Still the people remained at a distance,
while Moses approached the cloud where God was.

The word of the Lord.

---

106. **Dt 6:4-9**

Love the LORD, your God, with all your heart.

A reading from the Book of Deuteronomy

In those days
Moses said to the people:
"Hear, O Israel! The LORD is our God, the LORD alone!

Therefore, you shall love the LORD, your God,
with all your heart,
and with all your soul,
and with all your strength.
Take to heart these words which I enjoin on you today.
Drill them into your children.
Speak of them at home and abroad, whether you are busy or at rest.
Bind them at your wrist as a sign
and let them be as a pendant on your forehead.
Write them on the doorposts of your houses and on your gates."

The word of the Lord.

---

107. Dt 9:7-19

Your people have become depraved; they have already turned aside from the way I pointed out to them.

A reading from the Book of Deuteronomy

In those days,
Moses said to the people:
"Bear in mind and do not forget
how you angered the LORD, your God, in the desert.
From the day you left the land of Egypt
until you arrived in this place,
you have been rebellious toward the LORD.
At Horeb you so provoked the LORD
that he was angry enough to destroy you,
when I had gone up the mountain to receive
the stone tablets of the covenant
which the LORD made with you.
Meanwhile I stayed on the mountain forty days and forty nights

without eating or drinking,
till the Lord gave me the two tablets of stone
inscribed, by God's own finger, with a copy of all the words
that the Lord spoke to you on the mountain
from the midst of the fire on the day of the assembly.
Then, at the end of the forty days and forty nights,
when the Lord had given me the two stone tablets of the covenant, he said to me,
'Go down from here now, quickly,
for your people whom you have brought out of Egypt
have become depraved;
they have already turned aside from the way I pointed out to them
and have made for themselves a molten idol.
I have seen now how stiff-necked this people is,' the Lord said to me.
'Let me be, that I may destroy them
and blot out their name from under the heavens.
I will then make of you a nation mightier and greater than they.'

"When I had come down again from the blazing, fiery mountain,
with the two tablets of the covenant in both my hands,
I saw how you had sinned against the Lord, your God:
you had already turned aside from the way
which the Lord had pointed out to you
by making for yourselves a molten calf!
Raising the two tablets with both hands
I threw them from me and broke them before your eyes.

Then, as before, I lay prostrate before the LORD
for forty days and forty nights without eating or drinking,
because of all the sin you had committed in the sight of the LORD
and the evil you had done to provoke him.
For I dreaded the fierce anger of the LORD against you:
his wrath would destroy you.
Yet once again the LORD listened to me."

The word of the Lord.

---

108. Dt 30:15-20

Today I have set before you life
and prosperity, death and doom.

A reading from the Book of Deuteronomy

Moses said to the people:
"Today I have set before you
life and prosperity, death and doom.
If you obey the commandments of the LORD, your God,
which I enjoin on you today,
loving him, and walking in his ways,
and keeping his commandments, statutes and decrees,
you will live and grow numerous,
and the LORD, your God,
will bless you in the land you are entering to occupy.
If, however, you turn away your hearts and will not listen,
but are led astray and adore and serve other gods,
I tell you now that you will certainly perish;
you will not have a long life

on the land that you are crossing the Jordan to enter and occupy.
I call heaven and earth today to witness against you:
I have set before you life and death,
the blessing and the curse.
Choose life, then,
that you and your descendants may live, by loving the LORD, your God,
heeding his voice, and holding fast to him.
For that will mean life for you,
a long life for you to live on the land that the LORD swore
he would give to your fathers Abraham, Isaac and Jacob."

The word of the Lord.

---

109. 2 Sm 12:1-9, 13

David said to Nathan, "I have sinned against the LORD." Nathan answered David: "The LORD on his part has forgiven your sin: you shall not die."

A reading from the second Book of Samuel

In those days, the LORD sent Nathan to David, and when he came to him,
he said: "Judge this case for me!
In a certain town there were two men, one rich, the other poor.
The rich man had flocks and herds in great numbers.
But the poor man had nothing at all
except one little ewe lamb that he had bought.
He nourished her, and she grew up with him and his children.
She shared the little food he had
and drank from his cup and slept in his bosom.
She was like a daughter to him.

Now, the rich man received a visitor,
but he would not take from his own flocks and herds
to prepare a meal for the wayfarer who had come to him.
Instead he took the poor man's ewe lamb
and made a meal of it for his visitor."
David grew very angry with that man and said to Nathan:
"As the LORD lives, the man who has done this merits death!
He shall restore the ewe lamb fourfold
because he has done this and has had no pity."
Then Nathan said to David: "You are the man!
Thus says the LORD God of Israel:
'I anointed you king of Israel.
I rescued you from the hand of Saul.
I gave you your lord's house and your lord's wives for your own.
I gave you the house of Israel and of Judah.
And if this were not enough,
I could count up for you still more.
Why have you spurned the LORD
and done evil in his sight?
You have cut down Uriah the Hittite with the sword;
you took his wife as your own,
and him you killed with the sword of the Ammonites.' "

Then David said to Nathan, "I have sinned against the LORD."
Nathan answered David:
"The LORD on his part has forgiven your sin: you shall not die."

The word of the Lord.

110. Neh 9:1-20

The children of Israel gathered together fasting and confessed their sins.

A reading from the Book of Nehemiah

On the twenty-fourth day of this month,
the children of Israel gathered together fasting and in sackcloth,
their heads covered with dust.
Those descended from the children of Israel separated themselves
from all who were of foreign extraction,
then stood forward and confessed their sins
and the guilty deeds of their fathers.
When they had taken their places,
they read from the book of the law of the LORD their God,
for a fourth part of the day,
and during another fourth part they made their confession
and prostrated themselves before the LORD their God.
Standing on the platform of the Levites
were Jeshua, Binnui, Kadmiel, Shebaniah, Bunni, Sherebiah, Bani, and Chenani,
who cried out to the LORD their God, with a loud voice.
The Levites Jeshua, Kadmiel, Bani, Hashabneiah, Sherebiah, Hodiah, Shebaniah, and Pethahiah said,

"Arise, bless the LORD, your God,
from eternity to eternity!"

The children of Israel answered with the blessing,

"Blessed is your glorious name,
and exalted above all blessing and praise."

Then Ezra said: "It is you, O LORD,
you are the only one;
you made the heavens, the highest heavens and all their host,
the earth and all that is upon it,
the seas and all that is in them.
To all of them you give life,
and the heavenly hosts bow down before you.

"You, O LORD, are the God who chose Abram,
who brought him out from Ur of the Chaldees,
and named him Abraham.
When you had found his heart faithful in your sight,
you made the covenant with him to give to him and his posterity
the land of the Canaanites, Hittites, Amorites, Perizzites, Jebusites, and Girgashites.
These promises of yours you fulfilled, for you are just.

"You saw the affliction of our fathers in Egypt,
you heard their cry by the Red Sea;
You worked signs and wonders against Pharaoh,
against all his servants and the people of his land,
Because you knew of their insolence toward them;
thus you made for yourself a name even to this day.
The sea you divided before them,
on dry ground they passed through the midst of the sea;
Their pursuers you hurled into the depths,
like a stone into the mighty waters.
With a column of cloud you led them by day,
and by night with a column of fire,
To light the way of their journey,
the way in which they must travel.

On Mount Sinai you came down,
you spoke with them from heaven;
You gave them just ordinances, firm laws,
good statutes, and commandments;
Your holy sabbath you made known to them,
commandments, statutes, and law you prescribed for them,
by the hand of Moses your servant.
Food from heaven you gave them in their hunger,
water from a rock you sent them in their thirst.
You bade them enter and occupy the land
which you had sworn with upraised hand to give them.

"But they, our fathers, proved to be insolent;
they held their necks stiff
and would not obey your commandments.
They refused to obey and no longer remembered
the miracles you had worked for them.
They stiffened their necks and turned their heads
to return to their slavery in Egypt.
But you are a God of pardons,
gracious and compassionate, slow to anger and rich in mercy;
you did not forsake them.
Though they made for themselves a molten calf, and proclaimed,
'Here is your God who brought you up out of Egypt,'
and were guilty of great effronteries,
yet in your great mercy you did not forsake them in the desert.
The column of cloud did not cease to lead them by day on their journey,
nor did the column of fire by night cease to light for them
the way by which they were to travel.

"Your good spirit you bestowed on them,
to give them understanding;
your manna you did not withhold from their mouths,
and you gave them water in their thirst."

The word of the Lord.

---

111. Wis 1:1-16

Love justice because into a soul that plots evil wisdom enters not, nor dwells she in a body under debt of sin.

A reading from the Book of Wisdom

Love justice, you who judge the earth;
think of the LORD in goodness,
and seek him in integrity of heart;
Because he is found by those who test him not,
and he manifests himself to those who do not disbelieve him.
For perverse counsels separate a man from God,
and his power, put to the proof, rebukes the foolhardy;
Because into a soul that plots evil wisdom enters not,
nor dwells she in a body under debt of sin.
For the holy spirit of discipline flees deceit
and withdraws from senseless counsels;
and when injustice occurs it is rebuked.
For wisdom is a kindly spirit,
yet she acquits not the blasphemer of his guilty lips;
Because God is the witness of his inmost self
and the sure observer of his heart
and the listener to his tongue.
For the spirit of the LORD fills the world,
is all-embracing, and knows what man says.

Therefore no one who utters wicked things can go unnoticed,
nor will chastising condemnation pass him by.
For the devices of the wicked man shall be scrutinized,
and the sound of his words shall reach the LORD,
for the chastisement of his transgressions;
Because a jealous ear hearkens to everything,
and discordant grumblings are no secret.
Therefore guard against profitless grumbling,
and from calumny withhold your tongues;
For a stealthy utterance does not go unpunished,
and a lying mouth slays the soul.
Court not death by your erring way of life,
nor draw to yourselves destruction by the works of your hands.
Because God did not make death,
nor does he rejoice in the destruction of the living.
For he fashioned all things that they might have being;
and the creatures of the world are wholesome,
And there is not a destructive drug among them
nor any domain of the nether world on earth,
For justice is undying.

It was the wicked who with hands and words invited death,
considered it a friend, and pined for it,
and made a covenant with it,
Because they deserve to be in its possession.

The word of the Lord.

112. Wis 5:1-16

The hope of the wicked is like thistledown borne on the wind. But the just live forever.

A reading from the Book of Wisdom

Then shall the just one with great assurance confront
his oppressors who set at nought his labors.
Seeing this, they shall be shaken with dreadful fear,
and amazed at the unlooked-for salvation.
They shall say among themselves, rueful
and groaning through anguish of spirit:
"This is he whom once we held as a laughingstock
and as a type for mockery, fools that we were!
His life we accounted madness,
and his death dishonored.
See how he is accounted among the sons of God;
how his lot is with the saints!
We, then, have strayed from the way of truth,
and the light of justice did not shine for us,
and the sun did not rise for us.
We had our fill of the ways of mischief and of ruin;
we journeyed through impassable deserts,
but the way of the LORD we knew not.
What did our pride avail us?
What have wealth and its boastfulness afforded us?
All of them passed like a shadow
and like a fleeting rumor;
Like a ship traversing the heaving water,
of which, when it has passed, no trace can be found,
no path of its keel in the waves.
Or like a bird flying through the air;
no evidence of its course is to be found—

But the fluid air, lashed by the beat of pinions,
and cleft by the rushing force
Of speeding wings, is traversed:
and afterward no mark of passage can be found in it.
Or as, when an arrow has been shot at a mark,
the parted air straightway flows together again
so that none discerns the way it went through—
Even so we, once born, abruptly came to nought
and held no sign of virtue to display,
but were consumed in our wickedness."
Yes, the hope of the wicked is like thistledown borne on the wind,
and like fine, tempest-driven foam;
Like smoke scattered by the wind,
and like the passing memory of the nomad camping for a single day.
But the just live forever,
and in the LORD is their recompense,
and the thought of them is with the Most High.
Therefore shall they receive the splendid crown,
the beauteous diadem, from the hand of the LORD—
For he shall shelter them with his right hand,
and protect them with his arm.

The word of the Lord.

---

113. Sir 28:1-7

Forgive your neighbor's injustice; then when you pray, your own sins will be forgiven.

A reading from the Book of Sirach

The vengeful will suffer the LORD's vengeance,
for he remembers their sins in detail.
Forgive your neighbor's injustice;

then when you pray, your own sins will be forgiven.
Should a man nourish anger against his fellows
and expect healing from the LORD?
Should a man refuse mercy to his fellows,
yet seek pardon for his own sins?
If he who is but flesh cherishes wrath,
who will forgive his sins?
Remember your last days, set enmity aside;
remember death and decay, and cease from sin!
Think of the commandments, hate not your neighbor;
of the Most High's covenant, and overlook faults.

The word of the Lord.

---

114. Is 1:2-6, 15-18

Sons have I raised and reared,
but they have disowned me!

A reading from the Book of the Prophet Isaiah

Hear, O heavens, and listen, O earth,
for the LORD speaks:
Sons have I raised and reared,
but they have disowned me!
An ox knows its owner,
and an ass, its master's manger;
But Israel does not know,
my people has not understood.
Ah! sinful nation, people laden with wickedness,
evil race, corrupt children!
They have forsaken the LORD,
spurned the Holy One of Israel,
apostatized.
Where would you yet be struck,
you that rebel again and again?

The whole head is sick,
  the whole heart faint.
From the sole of the foot to the head
  there is no sound spot:
Wound and welt and gaping gash,
  not drained, or bandaged,
  or eased with salve.

When you spread out your hands,
  I close my eyes to you;
Though you pray the more,
  I will not listen.
Your hands are full of blood!
  Wash yourselves clean!
Put away your misdeeds from before my eyes;
  cease doing evil; learn to do good.
Make justice your aim: redress the wronged,
  hear the orphan's plea, defend the widow.

Come now, let us set things right,
  says the LORD:
Though your sins be like scarlet,
  they may become white as snow;
Though they be crimson red,
  they may become white as wool.

The word of the Lord.

---

115. Is 5:1-7

My friend had a vineyard. He looked for the crop of grapes, but what it yielded was wild grapes.

A reading from the Book of the Prophet Isaiah

Let me now sing of my friend,
  my friend's song concerning his vineyard.
My friend had a vineyard
  on a fertile hillside;

He spaded it, cleared it of stones,
and planted the choicest vines;
Within it he built a watchtower,
and hewed out a wine press.
Then he looked for the crop of grapes,
but what it yielded was wild grapes.

Now, inhabitants of Jerusalem and people of Judah,
judge between me and my vineyard:
What more was there to do for my vineyard
that I had not done?
Why, when I looked for the crop of grapes,
did it bring forth wild grapes?
Now, I will let you know
what I mean to do with my vineyard:
Take away its hedge, give it to grazing,
break through its wall, let it be trampled!
Yes, I will make it a ruin:
it shall not be pruned or hoed,
but overgrown with thorns and briers;
I will command the clouds
not to send rain upon it.
The vineyard of the LORD of hosts is the house of Israel,
and the people of Judah are his cherished plant;
He looked for judgment, but see, bloodshed!
for justice, but hark, the outcry!

The word of the Lord.

---

116. Is 43:22-28

It is I, I, who wipe out, for my own sake, your offenses.

A reading from the Book of the Prophet Isaiah

Thus says the LORD:
You did not call upon me, O Jacob,
for you grew weary of me, O Israel.

You did not bring me sheep for your burnt offerings,
nor honor me with your sacrifices.
I did not exact from you the service of offerings,
nor weary you for frankincense.
You did not buy me sweet cane for money,
nor fill me with the fat of your sacrifices;
Instead, you burdened me with your sins,
and wearied me with your crimes.
It is I, I, who wipe out,
for my own sake, your offenses;
your sins I remember no more.
Would you have me remember, have us come to trial?
Speak up, prove your innocence!
Your first father sinned;
your spokesmen rebelled against me
Till I repudiated the holy gates,
put Jacob under the ban,
and exposed Israel to scorn.

The word of the Lord.

---

117. Is 53:1-12

The LORD laid upon him the guilt of us all.

A reading from the Book of the Prophet Isaiah

Who would believe what we have heard?
To whom has the arm of the LORD been revealed?
He grew up like a sapling before him,
like a shoot from the parched earth;
There was in him no stately bearing to make us look at him,
nor appearance that would attract us to him.
He was spurned and avoided by people,
a man of suffering, accustomed to infirmity,

One of those from whom people hide their faces,
spurned, and we held him in no esteem.

Yet it was our infirmities that he bore,
our sufferings that he endured,
While we thought of him as stricken,
as one smitten by God and afflicted.
But he was pierced for our offenses,
crushed for our sins;
Upon him was the chastisement that makes us whole,
by his stripes we were healed.
We had all gone astray like sheep,
each following his own way;
But the LORD laid upon him
the guilt of us all.

Though he was harshly treated, he submitted
and opened not his mouth;
Like a lamb led to the slaughter
or a sheep before the shearers,
he was silent and opened not his mouth.
Oppressed and condemned, he was taken away,
and who would have thought any more of his destiny?
When he was cut off from the land of the living,
and smitten for the sin of his people,
A grave was assigned him among the wicked
and a burial place with evildoers,
Though he had done no wrong
nor spoken any falsehood.
But the LORD was pleased
to crush him in infirmity.

If he gives his life as an offering for sin,
he shall see his descendants in a long life,
and the will of the LORD shall be accomplished through him.

Because of his affliction
he shall see the light in fullness of days;
Through his suffering, my servant shall justify many,
and their guilt he shall bear.
Therefore I will give him his portion among the great,
and he shall divide the spoils with the mighty,
Because he surrendered himself to death
and was counted among the wicked;
And he shall take away the sins of many,
and win pardon for their offenses.

The word of the Lord.

---

118. Is 55:1-11

Let the scoundrel forsake his way, and the wicked man his thoughts; let him turn to the LORD for mercy; to our God, who is generous in forgiving.

A reading from the Book of the Prophet Isaiah

All you who are thirsty,
come to the water!
You who have no money,
come, receive grain and eat;
Come, without paying and without cost,
drink wine and milk!
Why spend your money for what is not bread,
your wages for what fails to satisfy?
Heed me, and you shall eat well,
you shall delight in rich fare.
Come to me heedfully,
listen, that you may have life.
I will renew with you the everlasting covenant,
the benefits assured to David.
As I made him a witness to the peoples,
a leader and commander of nations,
So shall you summon a nation you knew not,
and nations that knew you not shall run to you,

Because of the LORD, your God,
the Holy One of Israel, who has glorified you.

Seek the LORD while he may be found,
call him while he is near.
Let the scoundrel forsake his way,
and the wicked man his thoughts;
Let him turn to the LORD for mercy;
to our God, who is generous in forgiving.
For my thoughts are not your thoughts,
nor are your ways my ways, says the LORD.
As high as the heavens are above the earth,
so high are my ways above your ways
and my thoughts above your thoughts.

For just as from the heavens
the rain and snow come down
And do not return there
till they have watered the earth,
making it fertile and fruitful,
Giving seed to the one who sows
and bread to the one who eats,
So shall my word be
that goes forth from my mouth;
My word shall not return to me void,
but shall do my will,
achieving the end for which I sent it.

The word of the Lord.

---

119. Is 58:1-11

Then light shall rise for you in the darkness,
and the gloom shall become for you like midday.

A reading from the Book of the Prophet Isaiah

Thus says the LORD:
Cry out full-throated and unsparingly,
lift up your voice like a trumpet blast;

Tell my people their wickedness,
  and the house of Jacob their sins.
They seek me day after day,
  and desire to know my ways,
Like a nation that has done what is just
  and not abandoned the law of their God;
They ask me to declare what is due them,
  pleased to gain access to God.
"Why do we fast, and you do not see it?
  afflict ourselves, and you take no note of it?"

Lo, on your fast day you carry out your own pursuits,
  and drive all your laborers.
Yes, your fast ends in quarreling and fighting,
  striking with wicked claw.
Would that today you might fast
  so as to make your voice heard on high!
Is this the manner of fasting I wish,
  of keeping a day of penance:
That a man bow his head like a reed
  and lie in sackcloth and ashes?
Do you call this a fast,
  a day acceptable to the LORD?
This, rather, is the fasting that I wish:
  releasing those bound unjustly,
  untying the thongs of the yoke;
Setting free the oppressed,
  breaking every yoke;
Sharing your bread with the hungry,
  sheltering the oppressed and the homeless;
Clothing the naked when you see them,
  and not turning your back on your own.
Then your light shall break forth like the dawn,
  and your wound shall quickly be healed;
Your vindication shall go before you,
  and the glory of the LORD shall be your rear guard.

Then you shall call, and the LORD will answer,
  you shall cry for help, and he will say: Here I am!
If you remove from your midst oppression,
  false accusation and malicious speech;
If you bestow your bread on the hungry
  and satisfy the afflicted;
Then light shall rise for you in the darkness,
  and the gloom shall become for you like midday;
Then the LORD will guide you always
  and give you plenty even on the parched land.
He will renew your strength,
  and you shall be like a watered garden,
  like a spring whose water never fails.
  for the mouth of the LORD has spoken.

The word of the Lord.

---

120. Is 59:1-4, 9-15

It is your crimes that separate you from your God.

A reading from the Book of the Prophet Isaiah

Lo, the hand of the LORD is not too short to save,
  nor his ear too dull to hear.
Rather, it is your crimes
  that separate you from your God,
It is your sins that make him hide his face
  so that he will not hear you.
For your hands are stained with blood,
  your fingers with guilt;
Your lips speak falsehood,
  and your tongue utters deceit.
No one brings suit justly,
  no one pleads truthfully;
They trust in emptiness and tell lies;
  they conceive mischief and bring forth malice.

That is why right is far from us
  and justice does not reach us.
We look for light, and lo, darkness;
  for brightness, but we walk in gloom!
Like blind men we grope along the wall,
  like people without eyes we feel our way.
We stumble at midday as at dusk,
  in Stygian darkness, like the dead.
We all growl like bears,
  like doves we moan without ceasing.
We look for right, but it is not there;
  for salvation, and it is far from us.
For our offenses before you are many,
  our sins bear witness against us.
Yes, our offenses are present to us,
  and our crimes we know:
Transgressing, and denying the LORD,
  turning back from following our God,
Threatening outrage, and apostasy,
  uttering words of falsehood the heart has conceived.
Right is repelled,
  and justice stands far off;
For truth stumbles in the public square,
  uprightness cannot enter.
Honesty is lacking,
  and the man who turns from evil is despoiled.

The LORD saw this, and was aggrieved
  that right did not exist.

The word of the Lord.

121.

Jer 2:1-13

Two evils have my people done: they have forsaken me, the source of living waters; They have dug themselves cisterns, broken cisterns, that hold no water.

A reading from the Book of the Prophet Jeremiah

This word of the LORD came to me:
Go, cry out this message for Jerusalem to hear!

I remember the devotion of your youth,
how you loved me as a bride,
Following me in the desert,
in a land unsown.
Sacred to the LORD was Israel,
the first fruits of his harvest;
Should anyone presume to partake of them,
evil would befall him, says the LORD.

Listen to the word of the LORD, O house of Jacob!
All you clans of the house of Israel,
thus says the LORD:
What fault did your fathers find in me
that they withdrew from me,
Went after empty idols,
and became empty themselves?
They did not ask, "Where is the LORD
who brought us up from the land of Egypt,
Who led us through the desert,
through a land of wastes and gullies,
Through a land of drought and darkness,
through a land which no one crosses,
where no man dwells?"

When I brought you into the garden land
to eat its goodly fruits,
You entered and defiled my land,
you made my heritage loathsome.

The priests asked not,
  "Where is the LORD?"
Those who dealt with the law knew me not:
  the shepherds rebelled against me.
The prophets prophesied by Baal,
  and went after useless idols.
Therefore will I yet accuse you, says the LORD,
  and even your children's children I will accuse.
Pass over to the coast of the Kittim and see,
  send to Kedar and carefully inquire:
  Where has the like of this been done?
Does any other nation change its gods?—
  yet they are not gods at all!
But my people have changed their glory
  for useless things.
Be amazed at this, O heavens,
  and shudder with sheer horror, says the LORD.
Two evils have my people done:
  they have forsaken me, the source of living waters;
They have dug themselves cisterns,
  broken cisterns, that hold no water.

The word of the Lord.

---

122. Jer 7:21-26

Listen to my voice; then I will be your God and you shall be my people.

A reading from the Book of the Prophet Jeremiah

Thus says the LORD of hosts, the God of Israel:
  Heap your burnt offerings upon your sacrifices;
  eat up the flesh!
In speaking to your fathers
  on the day I brought them out of the land of Egypt,

I gave them no command concerning burnt
offering or sacrifice.
This rather is what I commanded them:
Listen to my voice;
then I will be your God
and you shall be my people.
Walk in all the ways that I command you,
so that you may prosper.

But they obeyed not,
nor did they pay heed.
They walked in the hardness of their evil hearts
and turned their backs, not their faces, to me.
From the day that your fathers left the land of Egypt
even to this day,
I have sent you untiringly all my servants the
prophets.
Yet they have not obeyed me nor paid heed;
they have stiffened their necks and done worse
than their fathers.

The word of the Lord.

---

123. Ez 11:14-21

I will remove the stony heart from their bodies,
and replace it with a natural heart, so that
they will live according to my statutes.

A reading from the Book of the Prophet Ezekiel

Thus the word of the LORD came to me:
Son of man, it is about your kinsmen,
your fellow exiles, and the whole house of Israel
that the inhabitants of Jerusalem say,
"They are far away from the LORD;
to us the land of Israel has been given as our
possession."

Therefore say: Thus says the Lord God:
Though I have removed them far among the nations
and scattered them over foreign countries—
and was for a while their only sanctuary
in the countries to which they had gone—
I will gather you from the nations
and assemble you from the countries over which you have been scattered,
and I will restore to you the land of Israel.
They shall return to it and remove from it all its detestable abominations.
I will give them a new heart and put a new spirit within them;
I will remove the stony heart from their bodies,
and replace it with a natural heart,
so that they will live according to my statutes,
and observe and carry out my ordinances;
thus they shall be my people and I will be their God.
But as for those whose hearts are devoted to their detestable abominations,
I will bring down their conduct upon their heads,
says the Lord God.

The word of the Lord.

---

124. Ez 18:20-32

If the wicked man turns away from all the sins he committed, he shall surely live, he shall not die.

A reading from the Book of the Prophet Ezekiel

The word of the Lord came to me thus:
Only the one who sins shall die.
The son shall not be charged with the guilt of his father,

nor shall the father be charged with the guilt of
his son.
The virtuous man's virtue shall be his own,
as the wicked man's wickedness shall be his own.
But if the wicked man turns away from all the sins
he committed,
if he keeps all my statutes and does what is right
and just,
he shall surely live, he shall not die.
None of the crimes he committed shall be remembered against him;
he shall live because of the virtue he has
practiced.
Do I indeed derive any pleasure from the death of
the wicked?
says the Lord God.
Do I not rather rejoice
when he turns from his evil way that he may live?
And if the virtuous man turns from the path of virtue
to do evil,
the same kind of abominable things that the
wicked man does,
can he do this and still live?
None of his virtuous deeds shall be remembered,
because he has broken faith and committed sin;
because of this, he shall die.
You say, "The Lord's way is not fair!"
Hear now, house of Israel:
Is it my way that is unfair,
or rather, are not your ways unfair?
When a virtuous man turns away from virtue to
commit iniquity, and dies,
it is because of the iniquity he committed that he
must die.
But if a wicked man, turning from the wickedness
he has committed,

does what is right and just,
he shall preserve his life;
since he has turned away from all the sins which he committed,
he shall surely live, he shall not die.
And yet the house of Israel says,
"The LORD's way is not fair!"
Is it my way that is not fair, house of Israel,
or rather, is it not that your ways are not fair?
Therefore I will judge you, house of Israel,
each one according to his ways, says the Lord GOD.
Turn and be converted from all your crimes,
that they may be no cause of guilt for you.
Cast away from you all the crimes you have committed,
and make for yourselves a new heart and a new spirit.
Why should you die, O house of Israel?
For I have no pleasure in the death of anyone who dies, says the Lord GOD.
Return and live!

The word of the Lord.

---

125. Ez 36:23-28

I will sprinkle clean water upon you and place a new spirit within you and make you live by my statutes.

A reading from the Book of the Prophet Ezekiel

Thus says the LORD:
I will prove the holiness of my great name,
profaned among the nations,
in whose midst you have profaned it.
Thus the nations shall know that I am the LORD, says the Lord GOD,

when in their sight I prove my holiness through
you.
For I will take you away from among the nations,
gather you from all the foreign lands,
and bring you back to your own land.
I will sprinkle clean water upon you
to cleanse you from all your impurities,
and from all your idols I will cleanse you.
I will give you a new heart and place a new spirit
within you,
taking from your bodies your stony hearts
and giving you natural hearts.
I will put my spirit within you and make you live by
my statutes,
careful to observe my decrees.
You shall live in the land I gave your fathers;
you shall be my people, and I will be your God.

The word of the Lord.

---

126. Hos 2:16-25

I will make a covenant for them on that day.

A reading from the Book of the Prophet Hosea

Thus says the LORD:
I will allure her;
I will lead her into the desert
and speak to her heart.
From there I will give her the vineyards she had,
and the valley of Achor as a door of hope.
She shall respond there as in the days of her youth,
when she came up from the land of Egypt.

On that day, says the LORD,
She shall call me "My husband,"
and never again "My baal."

Then will I remove from her mouth the names of the Baals,
so that they shall no longer be invoked.
I will make a covenant for them on that day,
with the beasts of the field,
With the birds of the air,
and with the things that crawl on the ground.
Bow and sword and war
I will destroy from the land,
and I will let them take their rest in security.
I will espouse you to me forever:
I will espouse you in right and in justice,
in love and in mercy;
I will espouse you in fidelity,
and you shall know the LORD.
On that day I will respond, says the LORD;
I will respond to the heavens,
and they shall respond to the earth;
The earth shall respond to the grain, and wine, and oil,
and these shall respond to Jezreel.
I will sow him for myself in the land,
and I will have pity on Lo-ruhama.
I will say to Lo-ammi, "You are my people,"
and he shall say, "My God!"

The word of the Lord.

---

127. Hos 11:1-11

I took them in my arms; I drew them with human cords.

A reading from the Book of the Prophet Hosea

Thus says the LORD:
When Israel was a child I loved him,
out of Egypt I called my son.
The more I called them,
the farther they went from me,

Sacrificing to the Baals
   and burning incense to idols.
Yet it was I who taught Ephraim to walk,
   who took them in my arms;
I drew them with human cords,
   with bands of love;
I fostered them like one
   who raises an infant to his cheeks;
Yet, though I stooped to feed my child,
   they did not know that I was their healer.

He shall return to the land of Egypt,
   and Assyria shall be his king;
The sword shall begin with his cities
   and end by consuming his solitudes.
Because they refused to repent,
   their own counsels shall devour them.
His people are in suspense about returning to him;
   and God, though in unison they cry out to him,
   shall not raise them up.

How could I give you up, O Ephraim,
   or deliver you up, O Israel?
How could I treat you as Admah,
   or make you like Zeboiim?
My heart is overwhelmed,
   my pity is stirred.
I will not give vent to my blazing anger,
   I will not destroy Ephraim again;
For I am God and not man,
   the Holy One present among you;
   I will not let the flames consume you.

They shall follow the LORD,
   who roars like a lion;
When he roars,
   his sons shall come frightened from the west,

Out of Egypt they shall come trembling, like sparrows,
from the land of Assyria, like doves;
And I will resettle them in their homes,
says the LORD.

The word of the Lord.

---

128. Hos 14:2-10

Return, O Israel, to the LORD, your God.

A reading from the Book of the Prophet Hosea

Thus says the LORD:
Return, O Israel, to the LORD, your God;
you have collapsed through your guilt.
Take with you words,
and return to the LORD;
Say to him, "Forgive all iniquity,
and receive what is good, that we may render
as offerings the bullocks from our stalls.
Assyria will not save us,
nor shall we have horses to mount;
We shall say no more, 'Our god,'
to the work of our hands;
for in you the orphan finds compassion."

I will heal their defection, says the LORD,
I will love them freely;
for my wrath is turned away from them.
I will be like the dew for Israel:
he shall blossom like the lily;
He shall strike root like the Lebanon cedar,
and put forth his shoots.
His splendor shall be like the olive tree
and his fragrance like the Lebanon cedar.
Again they shall dwell in his shade
and raise grain;

They shall blossom like the vine,
  and his fame shall be like the wine of Lebanon.

Ephraim! What more has he to do with idols?
  I have humbled him, but I will prosper him.
"I am like a verdant cypress tree"—
  Because of me you bear fruit!

Let him who is wise understand these things;
  let him who is prudent know them.
Straight are the paths of the LORD,
  in them the just walk,
  but sinners stumble in them.

The word of the Lord.

---

129. Jl 2:12-19

Return to me with your whole heart.

A reading from the Book of the Prophet Joel

Even now, says the LORD,
  return to me with your whole heart,
  with fasting, and weeping, and mourning;
Rend your hearts, not your garments,
  and return to the LORD, your God.
For gracious and merciful is he,
  slow to anger, rich in kindness,
  and relenting in punishment.
Perhaps he will again relent
  and leave behind him a blessing,
Offerings and libations
  for the LORD your God.

Blow the trumpet in Zion!
  proclaim a fast,
  call an assembly;
Gather the people,
  notify the congregation;

Assemble the elders,
  gather the children
  and the infants at the breast;
Let the bridegroom quit his room
  and the bride her chamber.
Between the porch and the altar
  let the priests, the ministers of the LORD, weep,
And say, "Spare, O LORD, your people,
  and make not your heritage a reproach,
  with the nations ruling over them!
Why should they say among the peoples,
  'Where is their God?' "

Then the LORD was stirred to concern for his land
  and took pity on his people.
The LORD answered and said to his people:
See, I will send you
  grain, and wine, and oil,
  and you shall be filled with them;
No more will I make you
  a reproach among the nations.

The word of the Lord.

---

130. Mic 6:1-15

Do the right and love goodness,
and walk humbly with your God.

A reading from the Book of the Prophet Micah

Hear, then, what the LORD says:
Arise, present your plea before the mountains,
  and let the hills hear your voice!
Hear, O mountains, the plea of the LORD,
  pay attention, O foundations of the earth!
For the LORD has a plea against his people,
  and he enters into trial with Israel.

O my people, what have I done to you,
or how have I wearied you? Answer me!
For I brought you up from the land of Egypt,
from the place of slavery I released you;
And I sent before you Moses,
Aaron, and Miriam.
My people, remember what Moab's King Balak planned,
and how Balaam, the son of Beor, answered him
. . . from Shittim to Gilgal,
that you may know the just deeds of the LORD.
With what shall I come before the LORD,
and bow before God most high?
Shall I come before him with burnt offerings,
with calves a year old?
Will the LORD be pleased with thousands of rams,
with myriad streams of oil?
Shall I give my first-born for my crime,
the fruit of my body for the sin of my soul?
You have been told, O man, what is good,
and what the LORD requires of you:
Only to do the right and to love goodness,
and to walk humbly with your God.

Hark! the LORD cries to the city.
(It is wisdom to fear your name!)
Hear, O tribe and city council,
You whose rich men are full of violence,
whose inhabitants speak falsehood
with deceitful tongues in their heads!
Am I to bear any longer criminal hoarding
and the meager ephah that is accursed?
Shall I acquit criminal balances,
bags of false weights?

Rather I will begin to strike you
with devastation because of your sins.

You shall sow, yet not reap,
  tread out the olive, yet pour no oil,
  and the grapes, yet drink no wine.
The word of the Lord.

---

131. Mic 7:2-7, 18-20

The Lord will again have compassion on us
and cast into the depths of the sea all our sins.

A reading from the Book of the Prophet Micah

The faithful are gone from the earth,
  among men the upright are no more!
They all lie in wait to shed blood,
  each one ensnares the other.
Their hands succeed at evil;
  the prince makes demands,
The judge is had for a price,
  the great man speaks as he pleases,
The best of them is like a brier,
  the most upright like a thorn hedge.
The day announced by your watchmen!
  your punishment has come;
  now is the time of your confusion.
Put no trust in a friend,
  have no confidence in a companion;
Against her who lies in your bosom
  guard the portals of your mouth.
For the son dishonors his father,
  the daughter rises up against her mother,
The daughter-in-law against her mother-in-law,
  and a man's enemies are those of his household.
But as for me, I will look to the Lord,
  I will put my trust in God my savior;
  my God will hear me!

Who is there like you, the God who removes guilt
and pardons sin for the remnant of his inheritance;
Who does not persist in anger forever,
but delights rather in clemency,
And will again have compassion on us,
treading underfoot our guilt?
You will cast into the depths of the sea
all our sins;
You will show faithfulness to Jacob,
and grace to Abraham,
As you have sworn to our fathers
from days of old.

The word of the Lord.

---

132. Zec 1:1-6

Return to me and I will return to you.

A reading from the
Book of the Prophet Zechariah

In the second year of Darius,
in the eighth month,
the word of the LORD came to the prophet Zechariah,
son of Berechiah, son of Iddo:
The LORD was indeed angry with your fathers...
and say to them:
Thus says the LORD of hosts:
Return to me, says the LORD of hosts,
and I will return to you, says the LORD of hosts.
Be not like your fathers whom the former prophets warned:
Thus says the LORD of hosts:
Turn from your evil ways and from your wicked deeds.

But they would not listen or pay attention to me,
says the LORD.
Your fathers, where are they?
And the prophets, can they live forever?
But my words and my decrees,
which I entrusted to my servants the prophets,
did not these overtake your fathers?
Then they repented and admitted:
"The LORD of hosts has treated us
according to our ways and deeds,
just as he had determined he would."

The word of the Lord.

RESPONSORIAL PSALMS

In longer Psalms, a selection of stanzas which form a coherent whole may be chosen instead of the entire Psalm.

133. Ps 13 (12):2-3, 4-5, 6

℟. (6a) I trust in your merciful love.

How long, O LORD? Will you forget me forever?
How long will you hide your face from me?
How long must I bear grief in my soul,
have sorrow in my heart all day long?
How long shall my enemy prevail over me?—℟.

Look, and answer me, O LORD my God!
Give light to my eyes lest I fall asleep in death;
lest my enemy say, "I have prevailed over him";
lest my foes rejoice when they see me fall.—℟.

As for me, I trust in your merciful love.
Let my heart rejoice in your salvation.
I will sing to the LORD who has been bountiful
with me.—℟.

---

134. Ps 25 (24):1b-3, 4-5, 6, 7, 8-9, 10-11, 12-14, 15-16, 17-18, 19-20, 21-22

℟. (16a) Turn to me, Lord, and have mercy on me.

To you, O LORD, I lift up my soul.
In you, O my God, I have trusted;
let me not be put to shame;
let not my enemies exult over me.
Let none who hope in you be put to shame;
but shamed are those who wantonly break faith.
—℟.

O LORD, make me know your ways.
Teach me your paths.
Guide me in your truth, and teach me;
for you are the God of my salvation.
I have hoped in you all day long.—℟.

Remember your compassion, O LORD,
and your merciful love,
for they are from of old.—℟.

Do not remember the sins of my youth,
nor my transgressions.
In your merciful love remember me,
because of your goodness, O LORD.—℟.

Good and upright is the LORD;
therefore he shows the way to sinners.
He guides the humble in right judgment;
to the humble he teaches his way.—℟.

All the LORD's paths are mercy and faithfulness,
for those who keep his covenant and commands.
O LORD, for the sake of your name,
forgive my guilt, for it is great.—℟.

Who is this that fears the LORD?
He will show him the path to choose.
His soul shall live in happiness,
and his descendants shall possess the land.

The LORD's secret is for those who fear him;
to them he reveals his covenant.—℟.

My eyes are always on the LORD,
for he rescues my feet from the snare.
Turn to me and have mercy on me,
for I am alone and poor.—℟.

Relieve the anguish of my heart,
and set me free from my distress.
See my lowliness and suffering,
and take away all my sins.—℟.

See how many are my foes:
with a violent hatred they hate me.
Preserve my life and rescue me.
Let me not be put to shame,
for in you I take refuge.—℟.

May integrity and virtue protect me,
for I have hoped in you, O LORD.
Grant redemption to Israel, O God,
from all its distress.—℟.

---

135. Ps 31 (30):2-3a, 3b-4, 5-6

℟. (6b) You will redeem us, O Lord, O faithful God.

In you, O LORD, I take refuge.
Let me never be put to shame.
In your justice, set me free;
incline your ear to me, and speedily rescue me.
—℟.

Be a rock of refuge for me,
a mighty stronghold to save me.
For you are my rock, my stronghold!
Lead me, guide me, for the sake of your name.—℟.

Release me from the snare they have hidden,
for you indeed are my refuge.

Into your hands I commend my spirit.
  You will redeem me, O LORD, O faithful God.—℟.

---

136. Ps 32 (31):1-2, 3-4, 5, 6, 7, 8, 9, 10, 11

℟. (5c) I will confess my transgression to the Lord.

Blessed is he whose transgression is forgiven,
  whose sin is remitted.
Blessed the man to whom the LORD imputes no guilt,
  in whose spirit is no guile.—℟.

I kept it secret and my frame was wasted.
  I groaned all day long,
For your hand, by day and by night,
  lay heavy upon me.
Indeed, my strength was dried up
  as by the summer's heat.—℟.

To you I have acknowledged my sin;
  my guilt I did not hide.
I said, "I will confess my transgression to the LORD."
  And you have forgiven the guilt of my sin.—℟.

So let each faithful one pray to you
  in the time of need.
The floods of water may reach high,
  but such a one they shall not reach.—℟.

You are a hiding place for me;
  you keep me safe from distress;
  you surround me with cries of deliverance.—℟.

I will instruct you and teach you
  the way you should go;
  I will fix my eyes upon you.—℟.

Be not like horse and mule, unintelligent,
  needing bridle and bit,
  or else they will not approach you.—℟.

Many sorrows has the wicked,
but loving mercy surrounds the one who trusts in the LORD.—℟.

Rejoice in the LORD, exult you just!
Ring out your joy, all you upright of heart!—℟.

---

137. Ps 36 (35):2, 3-4, 5, 6-7, 8, 9-10, 11-13

℟. (8) How precious is your mercy, O God!

Transgression speaks to the sinner
in the depths of his heart.
There is no fear of God before his eyes.—℟.

In his own eyes, he flatters himself,
not to see and detest his own guilt.
The words of his mouth are mischief and deceit.
He has ceased to be prudent and do good.—℟.

In bed he plots iniquity.
He sets his foot on every wicked way;
no evil does he reject.—℟.

Your mercy, LORD, reaches to heaven,
your truth to the clouds.
Your uprightness is like the mountains of God;
like the great deep, your justice.
Both man and beast you save, O LORD.—℟.

How precious is your mercy, O God!
The children of Adam seek shelter
in the shadow of your wings.—℟.

They feast on the riches of your house;
you give them drink from the stream of your delight.
For with you is the fountain of life,
and in your light we see light.—℟.

Maintain your mercy for those who know you,
your saving justice to upright hearts.

Let the foot of the proud not tread on me
  nor the hand of the wicked drive me out.
There have the evildoers fallen;
  flung down, unable to rise!—℟.

---

138. Ps 50 (49):7, 8 and 14-15, 16-17, 18-19, 20-21, 22-23

℟. (23b) To one whose way is blameless, I will show the salvation of God.

"Listen, my people, I will speak;
  Israel, I will testify against you,
  for I am God, your God."—℟.

"I do not rebuke you for your sacrifices;
  your offerings are always before me.
Give your praise as a sacrifice to God,
  and fulfill your vows to the Most High.
Then call on me in the day of distress.
  I will deliver you and you shall honor me."—℟.

But God will say to the wicked,
  "How can you recite my commandments,
and take my covenant on your lips,
  you who despise correction,
  and cast my words behind you?"—℟.

"You who see a thief and befriend him,
  who throw in your lot with adulterers,
who unbridle your mouth for evil,
  and yoke your tongue to deceit?"—℟.

"You who sit and malign your own brother,
  and slander your own mother's son?
You do this, and should I keep silence?
  Do you think that I am like you?
  I accuse you, lay the charge before you.—℟.

"Mark this, you who are forgetful of God,
  lest I seize you and none can deliver you.

A sacrifice of praise gives me honor,
 and to one whose way is blameless,
 I will show the salvation of God."—℟.

---

139. Ps 51 (50):3-4, 5-6, 7-9, 10-11, 12-13, 14-15, 16-17, 18-19, 20-21

℟. (14a) Restore in me the joy of your salvation.

Have mercy on me, O God,
 according to your merciful love;
according to your great compassion,
 blot out my transgressions.
Wash me completely from my iniquity,
 and cleanse me from my sin.—℟.

My transgressions, truly I know them;
 my sin is always before me.
Against you, you alone, have I sinned;
 what is evil in your sight I have done.
So you are just in your sentence,
 without reproach in your judgment.—℟.

Behold, in guilt I was born,
 a sinner when my mother conceived me.
Behold, you delight in sincerity of heart;
 in secret you teach me wisdom.
Cleanse me with hyssop, and I shall be pure;
 wash me, and I shall be whiter than snow.—℟.

Let me hear rejoicing and gladness,
 that the bones you have crushed may exult.
Turn away your face from my sins,
 and blot out all my guilt.—℟.

Create a pure heart for me, O God;
 renew a steadfast spirit within me.
Do not cast me away from your presence;
 take not your holy spirit from me.—℟.

Restore in me the joy of your salvation;
sustain in me a willing spirit.
I will teach transgressors your ways,
that sinners may return to you.—℟.

Rescue me from bloodshed, O God,
O God of my salvation,
and then my tongue shall ring out your justice.
O Lord, open my lips
and my mouth shall proclaim your praise.—℟.

For in sacrifice you take no delight;
burnt offering from me would not please you.
My sacrifice to God, a broken spirit:
a broken and humbled heart,
you will not spurn, O God.—℟.

In your good pleasure, show favor to Zion;
rebuild the walls of Jerusalem.
Then you will delight in right sacrifice,
burnt offerings wholly consumed.
Then you will be offered young bulls on your altar.—℟.

---

140. Ps 73 (72):1-3, 4-5, 6-7, 8-9, 10-12, 13-15, 16-17, 18-20, 21-22, 23-24, 25-26, 27-28

℟. (28a) For me to be near God is good.

How good is God to Israel,
to those who are pure of heart!
As for me, my feet came close to stumbling;
my steps had almost slipped,
for I was filled with envy of the proud,
when I saw how the wicked prosper.—℟.

For them there are no pains;
their bodies are sound and sleek.
They do not share in people's burdens;
they are not stricken like others.—℟.

So they wear their pride like a necklace;
they clothe themselves with violence.
With folds of fat, their eyes protrude.
With imagination their hearts overflow.—℟.

They scoff; they speak with malice.
From on high they threaten oppression.
They have set their mouths in the heavens,
and their tongues are roaming the earth.—℟.

So the people turn to them
and drink in all their words.
Thus they say, "How can God know?
Does the Most High have any knowledge?"
Look at them, such are the wicked;
ever prosperous, they grow in wealth.—℟.

How useless to keep my heart pure,
and wash my hands in innocence,
when I was stricken all day long,
suffered punishment with each new morning.
Then I said, "If I should speak like that,
I should betray your children's generation."—℟.

I strove to fathom this problem,
too hard for my mind to understand,
until I entered the holy place of God,
and came to discern their end.—℟.

How slippery the paths on which you set them;
you make them fall to destruction.
How suddenly they come to their ruin,
swept away, destroyed by terrors.
Like a dream one wakes from, O Lord,
when you wake you dismiss them as phantoms.—℟.

And so when my heart grew embittered,
and I was pierced to the depths of my being,
I was stupid and did not understand;
I was like a beast in your sight.—℟.

As for me, I was always in your presence;
you were holding me by my right hand.
By your counsel you will guide me,
and then you will lead me to glory.—℟.

What else have I in heaven but you?
Apart from you, I want nothing on earth.
My flesh and my heart waste away;
God is the strength of my heart,
my portion forever.—℟.

Surely, those who are far from you perish;
you put an end to all those who are unfaithful.
For me to be near God is good;
I have made the Lord God my refuge.
I will proclaim your works
at the gates of daughter Zion.—℟.

141. Ps 90 (89):1-2, 3-4, 5-6, 7-8, 9-10, 11-12, 13-15, 16-17

℟. (14) Fill us, O Lord, with your mercy, and we shall exult all our days.

O Lord, you have been our refuge,
from generation to generation.
Before the mountains were born,
or the earth or the world were brought forth,
you are God, from age to age.—℟.

You turn man back to dust,
and say, "Return, O children of Adam."
To your eyes a thousand years
are like yesterday, come and gone,
or like a watch in the night.—℟.

You sweep them away like a dream,
like grass which is fresh in the morning.

In the morning it sprouts and is fresh;
by evening it withers and fades.—℟.

Indeed, we are consumed by your anger;
we are struck with terror at your fury.
You have set our guilt before you,
our secret sins in the light of your face.—℟.

All our days pass away in your anger.
Our years are consumed like a sigh.
Seventy years is the span of our days,
or eighty if we are strong.
And most of these are toil and pain.
They pass swiftly and we are gone.—℟.

Who understands the power of your anger?
Your fury matches the fear of you.
Then teach us to number our days,
that we may gain wisdom of heart.—℟.

Turn back, O LORD! How long?
Show pity to your servants.
At dawn, fill us with your merciful love;
we shall exult and rejoice all our days.
Give us joy for the days of our affliction,
for the years when we looked upon evil.—℟.

Let your deed be seen by your servants,
and your glorious power by their children.
Let the favor of the LORD our God be upon us;
give success to the work of our hands.
O give success to the work of our hands.—℟.

---

142. Ps 95 (94):1-2, 3-5, 6-7b, 7c-9, 10-11

℟. (7c) O that today you would listen to the voice of the Lord!

Come, let us ring out our joy to the LORD;
hail the rock who saves us.

Let us come into his presence, giving thanks;
let us hail him with a song of praise.—℟.

A mighty God is the LORD,
a great king above all gods.
In his hand are the depths of the earth;
the heights of the mountains are his.
To him belongs the sea, for he made it,
and the dry land that he shaped by his hand.—℟.

O come; let us bow and bend low.
Let us kneel before the LORD who made us,
for he is our God, and we the people,
the people of his pasture, the flock of his hand.—℟.

O that today you would listen to his voice!
"Harden not your hearts as at Meribah,
as on that day at Massah in the desert
when your forebears put me to the test;
when they tried me, though they saw my work."
—℟.

"For forty years I abhorred that generation,
and I said, 'Their heart goes astray;
this people does not know my ways.'
Then I took an oath in my anger,
'Never shall they enter my rest.' "—℟.

---

143. Ps 119 (118):1 and 10-11, 12-13, 15-16

℟. (1) Blessed are those who walk in the law of the Lord.

Blessed are those whose way is blameless,
who walk in the law of the LORD!
I seek you with all my heart;
let me not stray from your commands.
I treasure your word in my heart,
lest I sin against you.—℟.

Blest are you, O Lord;
teach me your statutes.
With my lips have I recounted
all the decrees of your mouth.—℟.

I will ponder your precepts,
and consider your paths.
I take delight in your statutes;
I will not forget your word.—℟.

---

144. Ps 123 (122):1, 2, 3-4

℟. (2e) Our eyes are on the Lord our God.

To you have I lifted up my eyes,
you who dwell in the heavens.—℟.

Behold, like the eyes of slaves
on the hand of their lords,
like the eyes of a servant
on the hand of her mistress,
so our eyes are on the Lord our God,
till he show us his mercy.—℟.

Have mercy on us, Lord, have mercy.
We are filled with contempt.
Indeed, all too full is our soul
with the scorn of the arrogant,
the disdain of the proud.—℟.

---

145. Ps 130 (129):1-2, 3-4, 5-6b, 6c-8

℟. (7bc) With the Lord there is mercy, in him is plentiful redemption.

Out of the depths I cry to you, O Lord;
Lord, hear my voice!
O let your ears be attentive
to the sound of my pleadings.—℟.

If you, O LORD, should mark iniquities,
Lord, who could stand?
But with you is found forgiveness,
that you may be revered.—℟.

I long for you, O LORD,
my soul longs for his word.
My soul awaits the Lord
more than watchmen for daybreak.—℟.

More than watchmen for daybreak,
let Israel hope for the LORD.
For with the LORD there is mercy,
in him is plentiful redemption.
It is he who will redeem Israel
from all its iniquities.—℟.

---

146. Ps 139 (138):1-3, 4-6, 7-8, 9-10, 11-12, 13-14, 15, 16, 17-18, 23-24

℟. (23a) O search me, God, and know my heart.

O LORD, you search me and you know me.
You yourself know my resting and my rising;
you discern my thoughts from afar.
You mark when I walk or lie down;
you know all my ways through and through.—℟.

Before ever a word is on my tongue,
you know it, O LORD, through and through.
Behind and before, you besiege me,
your hand ever laid upon me.
Too wonderful for me, this knowledge;
too high, beyond my reach.—℟.

O where can I go from your spirit,
or where can I flee from your face?
If I climb the heavens, you are there.
If I lie in Sheol, you are there.—℟.

If I take the wings of the dawn
or dwell at the sea's furthest end,
even there your hand would lead me;
your right hand would hold me fast.—℟.

If I say, "Let the darkness hide me
and the light around me be night,"
even darkness is not dark to you,
the night shall be as bright as day,
and darkness the same as the light.—℟.

For it was you who formed my inmost being,
knit me together in my mother's womb.
I thank you who wonderfully made me;
how wonderful are your works,
which my soul knows well!—℟.

My frame was not hidden from you,
when I was being fashioned in secret
and molded in the depths of the earth.—℟.

Your eyes saw me yet unformed;
and all days are recorded in your book,
formed before one of them came into being.—℟.

To me how precious your thoughts, O God;
how great is the sum of them!
If I count them, they are more than the sand;
at the end I am still at your side.—℟.

O search me, God, and know my heart.
O test me, and know my thoughts.
See that my path is not wicked,
and lead me in the way everlasting.—℟.

---

147. Ps 143 (142):1-2, 3-4, 5-6, 7, 8, 9-10, 11

℟. (10) Teach me to do your will, my God.

Listen, O Lord, to my prayer;
turn your ear to my appeal.
You are faithful, you are just; give answer.

Do not call your servant to judgment,
for no one is righteous in your sight.—℟.

The foe has pursued my soul;
he has crushed my life to the ground.
He has made me dwell in darkness,
like those long dead.
Therefore my spirit fails;
my heart is desolate within me.—℟.

I remember the days that are past;
I ponder all your works.
I muse on what your hand has wrought,
and to you I stretch out my hands.
My soul is like a parched land before you.—℟.

O LORD, make haste and answer me,
for my spirit fails within me.
Do not hide your face from me,
lest I become like those going down to the pit.
—℟.

In the morning, let me hear your loving mercy,
for in you I place my trust.
Make me know the way I should walk;
to you I lift up my soul.—℟.

Rescue me, O LORD, from my foes;
to you have I fled for refuge.
Teach me to do your will,
for you are my God.
Let your good spirit guide me
upon ground that is level.—℟.

LORD, save my life for the sake of your name;
in your justice, lead my soul out of distress.—℟.

Readings from the New Testament

148. Rom 3:22-26

They are justified freely by his grace through the redemption in Christ Jesus.

A reading from the Letter of Saint Paul to the Romans

Brothers and sisters:
The righteousness of God through faith in Jesus Christ is
for all who believe.
For there is no distinction;
all have sinned and are deprived of the glory of God.
They are justified freely by his grace
through the redemption in Christ Jesus,
whom God set forth as an expiation,
through faith, by his Blood, to prove his righteousness
because of the forgiveness of sins previously committed,
through the forbearance of God—
to prove his righteousness in the present time,
that he might be righteous
and justify the one who has faith in Jesus.

The word of the Lord.

---

149. Rom 5:6-11

We boast of God through our Lord Jesus Christ, through whom we have now received reconciliation.

A reading from the Letter of Saint Paul to the Romans

Brothers and sisters:
Christ, while we were still helpless,
yet died at the appointed time for the ungodly.
Indeed, only with difficulty does one die for a just person,
though perhaps for a good person
one might even find courage to die.
But God proves his love for us
in that while we were still sinners Christ died for us.
How much more then, since we are now justified by his Blood,
will we be saved through him from the wrath.
Indeed, if, while we were enemies,
we were reconciled to God through the death of his Son,
how much more, once reconciled,
will we be saved by his life.
Not only that,
but we also boast of God through our Lord Jesus Christ,
through whom we have now received reconciliation.

The word of the Lord.

---

150. Rom 6:2-13

You must think of yourselves as being dead to sin and living for God in Christ Jesus.

A reading from the Letter of Saint Paul to the Romans

Brothers and sisters:
How can we who died to sin yet live in it?
Are you unaware that we who were baptized into Christ Jesus
were baptized into his death?

We were indeed buried with him through baptism into death,
so that, just as Christ was raised from the dead
by the glory of the Father,
we too might live in newness of life.

For if we have grown into union with him through a death like his,
we shall also be united with him in the resurrection.
We know that our old self was crucified with him,
so that our sinful body might be done away with,
that we might no longer be in slavery to sin.
For a dead person has been absolved from sin.
If, then, we have died with Christ,
we believe that we shall also live with him.
We know that Christ, raised from the dead, dies no more;
death no longer has power over him.
As to his death, he died to sin once and for all;
as to his life, he lives for God.
Consequently, you too must think of yourselves as being dead to sin
and living for God in Christ Jesus.
Therefore, sin must not reign over your mortal bodies
so that you obey their desires.
And do not present the parts of your bodies to sin
as weapons for wickedness,
but present yourselves to God as raised from the dead to life
and the parts of your bodies to God
as weapons for righteousness.

The word of the Lord.

151. Rom 6:16-23

For the wages of sin is death, but the gift of God is eternal life in Christ Jesus our Lord.

A reading from the Letter of Saint Paul to the Romans

Brothers and sisters:
Do you not know that if you present yourselves
to someone as obedient slaves,
you are slaves of the one you obey,
either of sin, which leads to death,
or of obedience, which leads to righteousness?
But thanks be to God that, although you were once slaves of sin,
you have become obedient from the heart
to the pattern of teaching to which you were entrusted.
Freed from sin, you have become slaves of righteousness.
I am speaking in human terms because of the weakness of your nature.
For just as you presented the parts of your bodies as slaves to impurity
and to lawlessness for lawlessness,
so now present them as slaves to righteousness for sanctification.
For when you were slaves of sin, you were free from righteousness.
But what profit did you get then
from the things of which you are now ashamed?
For the end of those things is death.
But now that you have been freed from sin and have become slaves of God,
the benefit that you have leads to sanctification,
and its end is eternal life.

For the wages of sin is death,
but the gift of God is eternal life in Christ Jesus our Lord.
The word of the Lord.

---

152. Rom 7:14-25

Miserable one that I am! Who will deliver me from this mortal body? Thanks be to God through Jesus Christ our Lord.

A reading from the Letter of Saint Paul to the Romans

Brothers and sisters:
We know that the law is spiritual;
but I am carnal, sold into slavery to sin.
What I do, I do not understand.
For I do not do what I want,
but I do what I hate.
Now if I do what I do not want,
I concur that the law is good.
So now it is no longer I who do it,
but sin that dwells in me.
I know that good does not dwell in me, that is, in my flesh.
The willing is ready at hand, but doing the good is not.
For I do not do the good I want,
but I do the evil I do not want.
Now if I do what I do not want, it is no longer I who do it,
but sin that dwells in me.
So, then, I discover the principle
that when I want to do right, evil is at hand.
For I take delight in the law of God, in my inner self,
but I see in my members another principle

at war with the law of my mind,
taking me captive to the law of sin that dwells in my members.
Miserable one that I am!
Who will deliver me from this mortal body?
Thanks be to God through Jesus Christ our Lord.
Therefore, I myself, with my mind, serve the law of God
but, with my flesh, the law of sin.

The word of the Lord.

---

153. Rom 12:1-2, 9-19 VT

Be transformed by the renewal of your mind.

A reading from the Letter of
Saint Paul to the Romans

I urge you, brothers and sisters, by the mercies of God,
to offer your bodies as a living sacrifice,
holy and pleasing to God, your spiritual worship.
Do not conform yourselves to this age
but be transformed by the renewal of your mind,
that you may discern what is the will of God,
what is good and pleasing and perfect.

Let love be sincere;
hate what is evil,
hold on to what is good;
love one another with mutual affection;
anticipate one another in showing honor.
Do not grow slack in zeal,
be fervent in spirit,
serve the Lord.
Rejoice in hope,
endure in affliction,
persevere in prayer.

Contribute to the needs of the holy ones,
exercise hospitality.
Bless those who persecute you,
bless and do not curse them.
Rejoice with those who rejoice,
weep with those who weep.
Have the same regard for one another;
do not be haughty but associate with the lowly;
do not be wise in your own estimation.
Do not repay anyone evil for evil;
be concerned for what is noble in the sight of all.
If possible, on your part, live at peace with all.
Beloved, do not look for revenge
but leave room for the wrath;
for it is written,
Vengeance is mine, I will repay, says the Lord.

The word of the Lord.

---

154. Rom 13:8-14

Throw off the works of darkness
and put on the armor of light.

A reading from the Letter of
Saint Paul to the Romans

Brothers and sisters:
Owe nothing to anyone, except to love one another;
for the one who loves another has fulfilled the law.
The commandments, *You shall not commit adultery; you shall not kill; you shall not steal; you shall not covet,*
and whatever other commandment there may be,
are summed up in this saying, namely,
You shall love your neighbor as yourself.
Love does no evil to the neighbor;
hence, love is the fulfillment of the law.

And do this because you know the time;
it is the hour now for you to awake from sleep.
For our salvation is nearer now than when we first believed;
the night is advanced, the day is at hand.
Let us then throw off the works of darkness
and put on the armor of light;
let us conduct ourselves properly as in the day,
not in orgies and drunkenness,
not in promiscuity and lust,
not in rivalry and jealousy.
But put on the Lord Jesus Christ,
and make no provision for the desires of the flesh.

The word of the Lord.

---

155. 2 Cor 5:17-21

God was reconciling the world to himself in Christ.

A reading from the second Letter of Saint Paul to the Corinthians

Brothers and sisters:
Whoever is in Christ is a new creation:
the old things have passed away;
behold, new things have come.
And all this is from God,
who has reconciled us to himself through Christ
and given us the ministry of reconciliation,
namely, God was reconciling the world to himself in Christ,
not counting their trespasses against them
and entrusting to us the message of reconciliation.
So we are ambassadors for Christ,
as if God were appealing through us.
We implore you on behalf of Christ,
be reconciled to God.

For our sake he made him to be sin who did not know sin,
so that we might become the righteousness of God in him.

The word of the Lord.

---

156. Gal 5:16-24

Those who belong to Christ Jesus have crucified their flesh with its passions and desires.

A reading from the Letter of Saint Paul to the Galatians

Brothers and sisters, live by the Spirit
and you will certainly not gratify the desire of the flesh.
For the flesh has desires against the Spirit,
and the Spirit against the flesh;
these are opposed to each other,
so that you may not do what you want.
But if you are guided by the Spirit, you are not under the law.
Now the works of the flesh are obvious:
immorality, impurity, lust, idolatry,
sorcery, hatreds, rivalry, jealousy,
outbursts of fury, acts of selfishness,
dissensions, factions, occasions of envy,
drinking bouts, orgies, and the like.
I warn you, as I warned you before,
that those who do such things will not inherit the Kingdom of God.
In contrast, the fruit of the Spirit is love, joy, peace,
patience, kindness, generosity,
faithfulness, gentleness, self-control.
Against such there is no law.

Now those who belong to Christ Jesus have crucified their flesh
with its passions and desires.

The word of the Lord.

---

157. Eph 2:1-10

God, because of the great love he had for us,
even when we were dead in our transgressions,
brought us to life with Christ.

A reading from the Letter of
Saint Paul to the Ephesians

Brothers and sisters:
You were dead in your transgressions and sins
in which you once lived following the age of this world,
following the ruler of the power of the air,
the spirit that is now at work in the disobedient.
All of us once lived among them in the desires of our flesh,
following the wishes of the flesh and the impulses,
and we were by nature children of wrath, like the rest.
But God, who is rich in mercy,
because of the great love he had for us,
even when we were dead in our transgressions,
brought us to life with Christ (by grace you have been saved),
raised us up with him,
and seated us with him in the heavens in Christ Jesus,
that in the ages to come
he might show the immeasurable riches of his grace
in his kindness to us in Christ Jesus.

For by grace you have been saved through faith,
and this is not from you; it is the gift of God;
it is not from works, so no one may boast.
For we are his handiwork, created in Christ Jesus for good works
that God has prepared in advance,
that we should live in them.

The word of the Lord.

---

158. Eph 4:1-3, 17-32

*Be renewed in the spirit of your minds,
and put on the new self.*

A reading from the Letter of Saint Paul to the Ephesians

I, then, a prisoner for the Lord,
urge you to live in a manner
worthy of the call you have received,
with all humility and gentleness,
with patience,
bearing with one another through love,
striving to preserve the unity of the spirit
through the bond of peace:

So I declare and testify in the Lord
that you must no longer live as the Gentiles do,
in the futility of their minds;
darkened in understanding,
alienated from the life of God because of their ignorance,
because of their hardness of heart,
they have become callous
and have handed themselves over to licentiousness
for the practice of every kind of impurity to excess.

That is not how you learned Christ,
assuming that you have heard of him
and were taught in him,
as truth is in Jesus,
that you should put away the old self of your former way of life,
corrupted through deceitful desires,
and be renewed in the spirit of your minds,
and put on the new self,
created in God's way in righteousness and holiness of truth.

Therefore, putting away falsehood,
speak the truth,
each one to his neighbor,
for we are members one of another.
Be angry but do not sin;
do not let the sun set on your anger,
and do not leave room for the Devil.
The thief must no longer steal,
but rather labor,
doing honest work with his own hands,
so that he may have something to share with one in need.
No foul language should come out of your mouths,
but only such as is good for needed edification,
that it may impart grace to those who hear.
And do not grieve the Holy Spirit of God,
with which you were sealed for the day of redemption.
All bitterness, fury, anger, shouting, and reviling
must be removed from you,
along with all malice.
And be kind to one another, compassionate,
forgiving one another as God has forgiven you in Christ.

The word of the Lord.

159. Eph 5:1-14

You were once darkness, but now you are light in the Lord. Live as children of light.

A reading from the Letter of Saint Paul to the Ephesians

Brothers and sisters:
Be imitators of God, as beloved children,
and live in love,
as Christ loved us and handed himself over for us
as a sacrificial offering to God for a fragrant aroma.
Immorality or any impurity or greed
must not even be mentioned among you,
as is fitting among holy ones,
no obscenity or silly or suggestive talk, which is out of place,
but instead, thanksgiving.
Be sure of this,
that no immoral or impure or greedy person, that is, an idolater,
has any inheritance in the Kingdom of Christ and of God.

Let no one deceive you with empty arguments,
for because of these things
the wrath of God is coming upon the disobedient.
So do not be associated with them.
For you were once darkness,
but now you are light in the Lord.
Live as children of light,
for light produces every kind of goodness and righteousness and truth.
Try to learn what is pleasing to the Lord.
Take no part in the fruitless works of darkness;
rather expose them,

for it is shameful even to mention the things done
by them in secret;
but everything exposed by the light becomes
visible,
for everything that becomes visible is light.
Therefore, it says:
"Awake, O sleeper,
and arise from the dead,
and Christ will give you light."

The word of the Lord.

---

160. Eph 6:10-18

Put on the armor of God, that you may be able to resist on the evil day.

A reading from the Letter of Saint Paul to the Ephesians

Brothers and sisters:
Draw your strength from the Lord and from his
mighty power.
Put on the armor of God so that you may be able to
stand firm
against the tactics of the Devil.
For our struggle is not with flesh and blood
but with the principalities, with the powers,
with the world rulers of this present darkness,
with the evil spirits in the heavens.
Therefore, put on the armor of God,
that you may be able to resist on the evil day
and, having done everything, to hold your ground.
So stand fast with your loins girded in truth,
clothed with righteousness as a breastplate,
and your feet shod in readiness for the Gospel of
peace.

In all circumstances, hold faith as a shield,
to quench all the flaming arrows of the Evil One.
And take the helmet of salvation and the sword of the Spirit,
which is the word of God.

With all prayer and supplication,
pray at every opportunity in the Spirit.
To that end, be watchful with all perseverance and supplication
for all the holy ones.

The word of the Lord.

---

161. Col 3:1-10, 12-17

If you were raised with Christ, seek what is above.
Put to death, then, the parts of you that are earthly.

A reading from the Letter of
Saint Paul to the Colossians

Brothers and sisters:
If you were raised with Christ, seek what is above,
where Christ is seated at the right hand of God.
Think of what is above, not of what is on earth.
For you have died, and your life is hidden with Christ in God.
When Christ your life appears,
then you too will appear with him in glory.

Put to death, then, the parts of you that are earthly:
immorality, impurity, passion, evil desire,
and the greed that is idolatry.
Because of these the wrath of God is coming upon the disobedient.
By these you too once conducted yourselves, when you lived in that way.

But now you must put them all away:
anger, fury, malice, slander,
and obscene language out of your mouths.
Stop lying to one another,
since you have taken off the old self with its practices
and have put on the new self,
which is being renewed, for knowledge,
in the image of its creator.

Put on, as God's chosen ones, holy and beloved,
heartfelt compassion, kindness, humility, gentleness, and patience,
bearing with one another and forgiving one another,
if one has a grievance against another;
as the Lord has forgiven you, so must you also do.
And over all these put on love,
that is, the bond of perfection.
And let the peace of Christ control your hearts,
the peace into which you were also called in one Body.
And be thankful.
Let the word of Christ dwell in you richly,
as in all wisdom you teach and admonish one another,
singing psalms, hymns, and spiritual songs
with gratitude in your hearts to God.
And whatever you do, in word or in deed,
do everything in the name of the Lord Jesus,
giving thanks to God the Father through him.

The word of the Lord.

162. Heb 12:1-5

In your struggle against sin you have not yet resisted to the point of shedding blood.

A reading from the Letter to the Hebrews

Brothers and sisters:
Since we are surrounded by so great a cloud of witnesses,
let us rid ourselves of every burden and sin that clings to us
and persevere in running the race that lies before us
while keeping our eyes fixed on Jesus,
the leader and perfecter of faith.
For the sake of the joy that lay before him
Jesus endured the cross, despising its shame,
and has taken his seat at the right of the throne of God.
Consider how he endured such opposition from sinners,
in order that you may not grow weary and lose heart.
In your struggle against sin
you have not yet resisted to the point of shedding blood.
You have also forgotten the exhortation addressed to you as sons:
My son, do not disdain the discipline of the Lord
or lose heart when reproved by him.

The word of the Lord.

---

163. Jas 1:22-27

Be doers of the word and not hearers only.

A reading from the Letter of Saint James

Beloved:
Be doers of the word and not hearers only, deluding yourselves.
For if anyone is a hearer of the word and not a doer,
he is like a man who looks at his own face in a mirror.
He sees himself, then goes off and promptly forgets
what he looked like.
But the one who peers into the perfect law of freedom and perseveres,
and is not a hearer who forgets but a doer who acts;
such a one shall be blessed in what he does.

If anyone thinks he is religious and does not bridle his tongue
but deceives his heart, his religion is vain.
Religion that is pure and undefiled before God and the Father is this:
to care for orphans and widows in their affliction
and to keep oneself unstained by the world.

The word of the Lord.

---

164. Jas 2:14-26

What good is it if someone says he has faith but does not have works?

A reading from the Letter of Saint James

What good is it, my brothers and sisters,
if someone says he has faith but does not have works?
Can that faith save him?
If a brother or sister has nothing to wear
and has no food for the day,
and one of you says to them,
"Go in peace, keep warm, and eat well,"

but you do not give them the necessities of the body,
what good is it?
So also faith of itself,
if it does not have works, is dead.

Indeed someone might say,
"You have faith and I have works."
Demonstrate your faith to me without works,
and I will demonstrate my faith to you from my works.
You believe that God is one.
You do well.
Even the demons believe that and tremble.
Do you want proof, you ignoramus,
that faith without works is useless?
Was not Abraham our father justified by works
when he offered his son Isaac upon the altar?
You see that faith was active along with his works,
and faith was completed by the works.
Thus the Scripture was fulfilled that says,
Abraham believed God,
and it was credited to him as righteousness,
and he was called *the friend of God.*
See how a person is justified by works and not by faith alone.
And in the same way, was not Rahab the harlot also justified by works
when she welcomed the messengers
and sent them out by a different route?
For just as a body without a spirit is dead,
so also faith without works is dead.

The word of the Lord.

165. Jas 3:1-12

If anyone does not fall short in speech,
he is a perfect man.

A reading from the Letter of Saint James

Not many of you should become teachers, my brothers and sisters,
for you realize that we will be judged more strictly,
for we all fall short in many respects.
If anyone does not fall short in speech, he is a perfect man,
able to bridle the whole body also.
If we put bits into the mouths of horses to make them obey us,
we also guide their whole bodies.
It is the same with ships:
even though they are so large and driven by fierce winds,
they are steered by a very small rudder
wherever the pilot's inclination wishes.
In the same way the tongue is a small member
and yet has great pretensions.

Consider how small a fire can set a huge forest ablaze.
The tongue is also a fire.
It exists among our members as a world of malice,
defiling the whole body
and setting the entire course of our lives on fire,
itself set on fire by Gehenna.
For every kind of beast and bird, of reptile and sea creature,
can be tamed and has been tamed by the human species,
but no man can tame the tongue.
It is a restless evil, full of deadly poison.

With it we bless the Lord and Father,
and with it we curse men
who are made in the likeness of God.
From the same mouth come blessing and cursing.

My brothers and sisters, this need not be so.
Does a spring gush forth from the same opening
both pure and brackish water?
Can a fig tree, my brothers and sisters, produce olives,
or a grapevine figs?
Neither can salt water yield fresh.

The word of the Lord.

---

166. 1 Pt 1:13-23

You were ransomed not with perishable things like silver or gold but with the precious Blood of Christ as of a spotless unblemished Lamb.

A reading from the first Letter of Saint Peter

Beloved:
Gird up the loins of your mind, live soberly,
and set your hopes completely on the grace to be brought to you
at the revelation of Jesus Christ.
Like obedient children,
do not act in compliance with the desires of your former ignorance
but, as he who called you is holy,
be holy yourselves in every aspect of your conduct,
for it is written, *Be holy because I am holy.*
Realize that you were ransomed from your futile conduct,
handed on by your ancestors,
not with perishable things like silver or gold
but with the precious Blood of Christ
as of a spotless unblemished Lamb.

He was known before the foundation of the world
  but revealed in the final time for you,
  who through him believe in God
  who raised him from the dead and gave him glory,
  so that your faith and hope are in God.

Since you have purified yourselves
  by obedience to the truth for sincere brotherly love,
  love one another intensely from a pure heart.
You have been born anew,
  not from perishable but from imperishable seed,
  through the living and abiding word of God.

The word of the Lord.

---

167. 2 Pt 1:3-11

Be all the more eager to make your call and election firm.

A reading from the second Letter of Saint Peter

Beloved:
His divine power has bestowed on us
  everything that makes for life and devotion,
  through the knowledge of him
  who called us by his own glory and power.
Through these, he has bestowed on us
  the precious and very great promises,
  so that through them you may come to share in
    the divine nature,
  after escaping from the corruption that is in the
    world
  because of evil desire.
For this very reason,
  make every effort to supplement your faith with
    virtue,
  virtue with knowledge, knowledge with self-control,
  self-control with endurance, endurance with
    devotion,

devotion with mutual affection, mutual affection
with love.
If these are yours and increase in abundance,
they will keep you from being idle or unfruitful
in the knowledge of our Lord Jesus Christ.
Anyone who lacks them is blind and shortsighted,
forgetful of the cleansing of his past sins.
Therefore, brothers and sisters, be all the more eager
to make your call and election firm,
for, in doing so, you will never stumble.
For, in this way, entry into the eternal Kingdom
of our Lord and savior Jesus Christ
will be richly provided for you.

The word of the Lord.

---

168. 1 Jn 1:5—2:2

If we acknowledge our sins, he is faithful and just and will forgive our sins and cleanse us from every wrongdoing.

A reading from the first Letter of Saint John

Beloved:
This is the message that we have heard from Jesus Christ
and proclaim to you: God is light,
and in him there is no darkness at all.
If we say, "We have fellowship with him,"
while we continue to walk in darkness,
we lie and do not act in truth.
But if we walk in the light as he is in the light,
then we have fellowship with one another,
and the Blood of his Son Jesus cleanses us from all sin.
If we say, "We are without sin," we deceive ourselves,
and the truth is not in us.

If we acknowledge our sins, he is faithful and just
and will forgive our sins and cleanse us from
every wrongdoing.
If we say, "We have not sinned," we make him a liar,
and his word is not in us.

My children, I am writing this to you so that you may
not commit sin.
But if anyone does sin, we have an Advocate with
the Father,
Jesus Christ the righteous one.
He is expiation for our sins,
and not for our sins only but for those of the
whole world.

The word of the Lord.

---

169. 1 Jn 2:3-11

Whoever hates his brother, is still in the darkness.

A reading from the first Letter of Saint John

Beloved:
The way we may be sure that we know Jesus
is to keep his commandments.
Whoever says, "I know him," but does not keep his
commandments
is a liar, and the truth is not in him.
But whoever keeps his word,
the love of God is truly perfected in him.
This is the way we may know that we are in union
with him:
whoever claims to abide in him ought to walk just
as he walked.

Beloved, I am writing no new commandment to you
but an old commandment that you had from the
beginning.

The old commandment is the word that you have heard.
And yet I do write a new commandment to you,
which holds true in him and among you,
for the darkness is passing away,
and the true light is already shining.
Whoever says he is in the light,
yet hates his brother, is still in the darkness.
Whoever loves his brother remains in the light,
and there is nothing in him to cause a fall.
Whoever hates his brother is in darkness;
he walks in darkness
and does not know where he is going
because the darkness has blinded his eyes.

The word of the Lord.

---

170. 1 Jn 3:1-24

We know that we have passed from death to life because we love our brothers.

A reading from the first Letter of Saint John

See what love the Father has bestowed on us
that we may be called the children of God.
Yet so we are.
The reason the world does not know us
is that it did not know him.
Beloved, we are God's children now;
what we shall be has not yet been revealed.
We do know that when it is revealed
we shall be like him,
for we shall see him as he is.
Everyone who has this hope based on him makes himself pure,
as he is pure.

Everyone who commits sin commits lawlessness,
for sin is lawlessness.
You know that he was revealed to take away sins,
and in him there is no sin.
No one who remains in him sins;
no one who sins has seen him or known him.
Children, let no one deceive you.
The person who acts in righteousness is righteous,
just as he is righteous.
Whoever sins belongs to the Devil,
because the Devil has sinned from the beginning.
Indeed, the Son of God was revealed to destroy the works of the Devil.
No one who is begotten by God commits sin,
because God's seed remains in him;
he cannot sin because he is begotten by God.
In this way, the children of God and the children of the Devil are made plain;
no one who fails to act in righteousness belongs to God,
nor anyone who does not love his brother.

For this is the message you have heard from the beginning:
we should love one another,
unlike Cain who belonged to the Evil One and slaughtered his brother.
Why did he slaughter him?
Because his own works were evil,
and those of his brother righteous.
Do not be amazed, then, brothers and sisters,
if the world hates you.
We know that we have passed from death to life
because we love our brothers.
Whoever does not love remains in death.

Everyone who hates his brother is a murderer,
and you know that no murderer has eternal life remaining in him.
The way we came to know love
was that he laid down his life for us;
so we ought to lay down our lives for our brothers.
If someone who has worldly means sees a brother in need
and refuses him compassion, how can the love of God remain in him?
Children, let us love not in word or speech but in deed and truth.
Now this is how we shall know that we belong to the truth
and reassure our hearts before him in whatever our hearts condemn,
for God is greater than our hearts and knows everything.
Beloved, if our hearts do not condemn us,
we have confidence in God
and receive from him whatever we ask,
because we keep his commandments and do what pleases him.
And his commandment is this:
we should believe in the name of his Son, Jesus Christ,
and love one another just as he commanded us.
Those who keep his commandments remain in him, and he in them,
and the way we know that he remains in us
is from the Spirit that he gave us.

The word of the Lord.

171. 1 Jn 4:16-21

God is love, and whoever remains in love remains in God and God in him.

A reading from the first Letter of Saint John

Beloved:
We have come to know and to believe in the love God has for us.

God is love, and whoever remains in love remains in God and God in him.
In this is love brought to perfection among us,
that we have confidence on the day of judgment
because as he is, so are we in this world.
There is no fear in love,
but perfect love drives out fear
because fear has to do with punishment,
and so one who fears is not yet perfect in love.
Beloved, we love God because
he first loved us.
If anyone says, "I love God,"
but hates his brother, he is a liar;
for whoever does not love a brother whom he has seen
cannot love God whom he has not seen.
This is the commandment we have from him:
Whoever loves God must also love his brother.

The word of the Lord.

---

172. Rev 2:1-5

A reading from the Book of Revelation

Repent, and do the works you did at first.

"To the angel of the Church in Ephesus, write this:

" 'The one who holds the seven stars in his right hand

and walks in the midst of the seven gold lamp-
stands says this:
"I know your works, your labor, and your endurance,
and that you cannot tolerate the wicked;
you have tested those who call themselves apostles but are not,
and discovered that they are impostors.
Moreover, you have endurance and have suffered for my name,
and you have not grown weary.
Yet I hold this against you:
you have lost the love you had at first.
Realize how far you have fallen.
Repent, and do the works you did at first.
Otherwise, I will come to you and remove your lampstand from its place,
unless you repent." ' "

The word of the Lord.

---

173. Rev 3:14-22

Because you are lukewarm, neither hot nor cold,
I will spit you out of my mouth.

A reading from the Book of Revelation

"To the angel of the Church in Laodicea, write this:

" 'The Amen, the faithful and true witness,
the source of God's creation, says this:
"I know your works;
I know that you are neither cold nor hot.
I wish you were either cold or hot.
So, because you are lukewarm, neither hot nor cold,
I will spit you out of my mouth.
For you say, 'I am rich and affluent and have no need of anything,'

and yet do not realize that you are wretched,
pitiable, poor, blind, and naked.
I advise you to buy from me gold refined by fire so
that you may be rich,
and white garments to put on
so that your shameful nakedness may not be
exposed,
and buy ointment to smear on your eyes so that
you may see.
Those whom I love, I reprove and chastise.
Be earnest, therefore, and repent.

" ' "Behold, I stand at the door and knock.
If anyone hears my voice and opens the door,
then I will enter his house and dine with him,
and he with me.
I will give the victor the right to sit with me on my
throne,
as I myself first won the victory
and sit with my Father on his throne.

" ' "Whoever has ears ought to hear
what the Spirit says to the churches." ' "

The word of the Lord.

---

174. Rev 20:11-15

All the dead were judged according to their deeds.

A reading from the Book of Revelation

Next I saw a large white throne and the one who
was sitting on it.
The earth and the sky fled from his presence
and there was no place for them.
I saw the dead, the great and the lowly, standing
before the throne,
and scrolls were opened.

Then another scroll was opened, the book of life.
The dead were judged according to their deeds,
by what was written in the scrolls.
The sea gave up its dead;
then Death and Hades gave up their dead.
All the dead were judged according to their deeds.
Then Death and Hades were thrown into the pool of fire.
(This pool of fire is the second death.)
Anyone whose name was not found written in the book of life
was thrown into the pool of fire.

The word of the Lord.

---

175. Rev 21:1-8

The victor will inherit these gifts, and I shall be his God, and he will be my son.

A reading from the Book of Revelation

I, John, saw a new heaven and a new earth.
The former heaven and the former earth had passed away,
and the sea was no more.
I also saw the holy city, a new Jerusalem,
coming down out of heaven from God,
prepared as a bride adorned for her husband.
I heard a loud voice from the throne saying,
"Behold, God's dwelling is with the human race.
He will dwell with them and they will be his people
and God himself will always be with them as their God.
He will wipe every tear from their eyes,
and there shall be no more death or mourning, wailing or pain,
for the old order has passed away."

The one who sat on the throne said,
"Behold, I make all things new."
Then he said, "Write these words down,
for they are trustworthy and true."
He said to me, "They are accomplished.
I am the Alpha and the Omega,
the beginning and the end.
To the thirsty I will give a gift
from the spring of life-giving water.
The victor will inherit these gifts,
and I shall be his God,
and he will be my son.
But as for cowards, the unfaithful, the depraved,
murderers, the unchaste, sorcerers, idol-worshipers,
and deceivers of every sort,
their lot is in the burning pool of fire and sulfur,
which is the second death."

The word of the Lord.

Gospel Readings

176. Mt 3:1-12

Repent, for the Kingdom of heaven is at hand!

✠ A reading from the holy Gospel according to Matthew

John the Baptist appeared, preaching in the desert of Judea
and saying, "Repent, for the Kingdom of heaven is at hand!"
It was of him that the prophet Isaiah had spoken when he said:
A voice of one crying out in the desert,
Prepare the way of the Lord,
make straight his paths.

John wore clothing made of camel's hair
and had a leather belt around his waist.
His food was locusts and wild honey.
At that time Jerusalem, all Judea,
and the whole region around the Jordan
were going out to him
and were being baptized by him in the Jordan River
as they acknowledged their sins.

When he saw many of the Pharisees and Sadducees coming to his baptism, he said to them, "You brood of vipers!
Who warned you to flee from the coming wrath?
Produce good fruit as evidence of your repentance.
And do not presume to say to yourselves,
'We have Abraham as our father.'
For I tell you,
God can raise up children to Abraham from these stones.
Even now the ax lies at the root of the trees.
Therefore every tree that does not bear good fruit
will be cut down and thrown into the fire.
I am baptizing you with water, for repentance,
but the one who is coming after me is mightier than I.
I am not worthy to carry his sandals.
He will baptize you with the Holy Spirit and fire.
His winnowing fan is in his hand.
He will clear his threshing floor
and gather his wheat into his barn,
but the chaff he will burn with unquenchable fire."

The Gospel of the Lord.

177. Mt 4:12-17

Repent, for the Kingdom of heaven is at hand.

✠ A reading from the holy Gospel according to Matthew

When Jesus heard that John had been arrested,
he withdrew to Galilee.
He left Nazareth and went to live in Capernaum by the sea,
in the region of Zebulun and Naphtali,
that what had been said through Isaiah the prophet might be fulfilled:

Land of Zebulun and land of Naphtali,
the way to the sea, beyond the Jordan,
Galilee of the Gentiles,
the people who sit in darkness
have seen a great light,
on those dwelling in a land overshadowed by death
light has arisen.

From that time on, Jesus began to preach and say,
"Repent, for the Kingdom of heaven is at hand."

The Gospel of the Lord.

---

178. Mt 5:1-12

When Jesus saw the crowds, he went up the mountain, and his disciples came to him.

✠ A reading from the holy Gospel according to Matthew

When Jesus saw the crowds, he went up the mountain,
and after he had sat down, his disciples came to him.

He began to teach them, saying:
"Blessed are the poor in spirit,
for theirs is the Kingdom of heaven.
Blessed are they who mourn,
for they will be comforted.
Blessed are the meek,
for they will inherit the land.
Blessed are they who hunger and thirst for righteousness,
for they will be satisfied.
Blessed are the merciful,
for they will be shown mercy.
Blessed are the clean of heart,
for they will see God.
Blessed are the peacemakers,
for they will be called children of God.
Blessed are they who are persecuted for the sake of righteousness,
for theirs is the Kingdom of heaven.
Blessed are you when they insult you and persecute you
and utter every kind of evil against you falsely because of me.
Rejoice and be glad,
for your reward will be great in heaven.
Thus they persecuted the prophets who were before you."

The Gospel of the Lord.

---

179. Mt 5:13-16

Your light must shine before others.

✠ A reading from the holy Gospel
according to Matthew

Jesus said to his disciples:
"You are the salt of the earth.
But if salt loses its taste, with what can it be seasoned?
It is no longer good for anything
but to be thrown out and trampled underfoot.
You are the light of the world.
A city set on a mountain cannot be hidden.
Nor do they light a lamp and then put it under a bushel basket;
it is set on a lampstand,
where it gives light to all in the house.
Just so, your light must shine before others,
that they may see your good deeds
and glorify your heavenly Father."

The Gospel of the Lord.

---

180. Mt 5:17-47

But I say to you.

✠ A reading from the holy Gospel according to Matthew

Jesus said to his disciples:
"Do not think that I have come to abolish the law or the prophets.
I have come not to abolish but to fulfill.
Amen, I say to you, until heaven and earth pass away,
not the smallest letter or the smallest part of a letter
will pass from the law,
until all things have taken place.
Therefore, whoever breaks one of the least of these commandments
and teaches others to do so
will be called least in the Kingdom of heaven.

But whoever obeys and teaches these commandments
will be called greatest in the Kingdom of heaven.
I tell you, unless your righteousness surpasses
that of the scribes and Pharisees,
you will not enter the Kingdom of heaven.

"You have heard that it was said to your ancestors,
You shall not kill; and whoever kills will be liable to judgment.
But I say to you,
whoever is angry with his brother
will be liable to judgment;
and whoever says to his brother, *Raqa*,
will be answerable to the Sanhedrin;
and whoever says, 'You fool,'
will be liable to fiery Gehenna.
Therefore, if you bring your gift to the altar,
and there recall that your brother
has anything against you,
leave your gift there at the altar,
go first and be reconciled with your brother,
and then come and offer your gift.
Settle with your opponent quickly while on the way to court.
Otherwise your opponent will hand you over to the judge,
and the judge will hand you over to the guard,
and you will be thrown into prison.
Amen, I say to you,
you will not be released until you have paid the last penny.

"You have heard that it was said,
You shall not commit adultery.
But I say to you,
everyone who looks at a woman with lust

has already committed adultery with her in his heart.
If your right eye causes you to sin,
tear it out and throw it away.
It is better for you to lose one of your members
than to have your whole body thrown into Gehenna.
And if your right hand causes you to sin,
cut it off and throw it away.
It is better for you to lose one of your members
than to have your whole body go into Gehenna.

"It was also said,
Whoever divorces his wife must give her a bill of divorce.
But I say to you,
whoever divorces his wife—unless the marriage is unlawful—
causes her to commit adultery,
and whoever marries a divorced woman commits adultery.

"Again you have heard that it was said to your ancestors,
Do not take a false oath,
but make good to the Lord all that you vow.
But I say to you, do not swear at all;
not by heaven, for it is God's throne;
nor by the earth, for it is his footstool;
nor by Jerusalem, for it is the city of the great King.
Do not swear by your head,
for you cannot make a single hair white or black.
Let your 'Yes' mean 'Yes,' and your 'No' mean 'No.'
Anything more is from the Evil One."

"You have heard that it was said,
An eye for an eye and a tooth for a tooth.

But I say to you, offer no resistance to one who is evil.
When someone strikes you on your right cheek,
turn the other one as well.
If anyone wants to go to law with you over your tunic,
hand over your cloak as well.
Should anyone press you into service for one mile,
go for two miles.
Give to the one who asks of you,
and do not turn your back on one who wants to borrow.

"You have heard that it was said,
You shall love your neighbor and hate your enemy.
But I say to you, love your enemies
and pray for those who persecute you,
that you may be children of your heavenly Father,
for he makes his sun rise on the bad and the good,
and causes rain to fall on the just and the unjust.
For if you love those who love you, what recompense will you have?
Do not the tax collectors do the same?
And if you greet your brothers only,
what is unusual about that?
Do not the pagans do the same?"

The Gospel of the Lord.

---

181. Mt 9:1-8

Courage, child, your sins are forgiven.

✠ A reading from the holy Gospel according to Matthew

After entering a boat, Jesus made the crossing, and came into his own town.

And there people brought to him a paralytic lying on
a stretcher.
When Jesus saw their faith, he said to the paralytic,
"Courage, child, your sins are forgiven."
At that, some of the scribes said to themselves,
"This man is blaspheming."
Jesus knew what they were thinking, and said,
"Why do you harbor evil thoughts?
Which is easier, to say, 'Your sins are forgiven,'
or to say, 'Rise and walk'?
But that you may know that the Son of Man
has authority on earth to forgive sins"—
he then said to the paralytic,
"Rise, pick up your stretcher, and go home."
He rose and went home.
When the crowds saw this they were struck with awe
and glorified God who had given such authority
to men.

The Gospel of the Lord.

---

182. Mt 9:9-13

I did not come to call the righteous but sinners.

✠ A reading from the holy Gospel
according to Matthew

As Jesus passed on from there,
he saw a man named Matthew sitting at the
customs post.
He said to him, "Follow me."
And he got up and followed him.
While he was at table in his house,
many tax collectors and sinners came
and sat with Jesus and his disciples.
The Pharisees saw this and said to his disciples,
"Why does your teacher eat with tax collectors
and sinners?"

He heard this and said,
"Those who are well do not need a physician, but the sick do.
Go and learn the meaning of the words,
I desire mercy, not sacrifice.
I did not come to call the righteous but sinners."

The Gospel of the Lord.

---

183. Mt 18:15-20

You have won over your brother.

✠ A reading from the holy Gospel according to Matthew

Jesus said to his disciples:
"If your brother sins against you,
go and tell him his fault between you and him alone.
If he listens to you, you have won over your brother.
If he does not listen,
take one or two others along with you,
so that every fact may be established
on the testimony of two or three witnesses.
If he refuses to listen to them, tell the Church.
If he refuses to listen even to the Church,
then treat him as you would a Gentile or a tax collector.
Amen, I say to you,
whatever you bind on earth shall be bound in heaven,
and whatever you loose on earth shall be loosed in heaven.
Again, amen, I say to you, if two of you agree on earth
about anything for which they are to pray,
it shall be granted to them by my heavenly Father.

For where two or three are gathered together in my name,
there am I in the midst of them."

The Gospel of the Lord.

---

184. Mt 18:21-35

So will my heavenly Father do to you, unless each of you forgives your brother from your heart.

✠ A reading from the holy Gospel according to Matthew

Peter approached Jesus and asked him,
"Lord, if my brother sins against me,
how often must I forgive him?
As many as seven times?"
Jesus answered, "I say to you, not seven times but seventy-seven times.
That is why the Kingdom of heaven may be likened to a king
who decided to settle accounts with his servants.
When he began the accounting,
a debtor was brought before him who owed him a huge amount.
Since he had no way of paying it back,
his master ordered him to be sold,
along with his wife, his children, and all his property,
in payment of the debt.
At that, the servant fell down, did him homage, and said,
'Be patient with me, and I will pay you back in full.'
Moved with compassion the master of that servant
let him go and forgave him the loan.
When that servant had left, he found one of his fellow servants
who owed him a much smaller amount.

He seized him and started to choke him, demanding,
'Pay back what you owe.'
Falling to his knees, his fellow servant begged him,
'Be patient with me, and I will pay you back.'
But he refused.
Instead, he had him put in prison
until he paid back the debt.
Now when his fellow servants saw what had happened,
they were deeply disturbed, and went to their master
and reported the whole affair.
His master summoned him and said to him, 'You wicked servant!
I forgave you your entire debt because you begged me to.
Should you not have had pity on your fellow servant,
as I had pity on you?'
Then in anger his master handed him over to the torturers
until he should pay back the whole debt.
So will my heavenly Father do to you,
unless each of you forgives your brother from your heart."

The Gospel of the Lord.

---

185. Mt 25:31-46

Whatever you did for one of these least brothers of mine, you did for me.

✠ A reading from the holy Gospel according to Matthew

Jesus said to his disciples:
"When the Son of Man comes in his glory,
and all the angels with him,

he will sit upon his glorious throne,
and all the nations will be assembled before him.
And he will separate them one from another,
as a shepherd separates the sheep from the goats.
He will place the sheep on his right and the goats on his left.
Then the king will say to those on his right,
'Come, you who are blessed by my Father.
Inherit the kingdom prepared for you from the foundation of the world.
For I was hungry and you gave me food,
I was thirsty and you gave me drink,
a stranger and you welcomed me,
naked and you clothed me,
ill and you cared for me,
in prison and you visited me.'
Then the righteous will answer him and say,
'Lord, when did we see you hungry and feed you,
or thirsty and give you drink?
When did we see you a stranger and welcome you,
or naked and clothe you?
When did we see you ill or in prison, and visit you?'
And the king will say to them in reply,
'Amen, I say to you, whatever you did
for one of these least brothers of mine, you did for me.'
Then he will say to those on his left,
'Depart from me, you accursed,
into the eternal fire prepared for the Devil and his angels.
For I was hungry and you gave me no food,
I was thirsty and you gave me no drink,
a stranger and you gave me no welcome,
naked and you gave me no clothing,
ill and in prison, and you did not care for me.'

Then they will answer and say,
'Lord, when did we see you hungry or thirsty
or a stranger or naked or ill or in prison,
and not minister to your needs?'
He will answer them, 'Amen, I say to you,
what you did not do for one of these least ones,
you did not do for me.'
And these will go off to eternal punishment,
but the righteous to eternal life."

The Gospel of the Lord.

---

186. Mt 26:69-75

He went out and began to weep bitterly.

✠ A reading from the holy Gospel
according to Matthew

Now Peter was sitting outside in the courtyard.
One of the maids came over to him and said,
"You too were with Jesus the Galilean."
But he denied it in front of everyone, saying,
"I do not know what you are talking about!"
As he went out to the gate, another girl saw him
and said to those who were there,
"This man was with Jesus the Nazorean."
Again he denied it with an oath,
"I do not know the man!"
A little later the bystanders came over and said to Peter,
"Surely you too are one of them;
even your speech gives you away."
At that he began to curse and to swear,
"I do not know the man."
And immediately a cock crowed.
Then Peter remembered the word that Jesus had spoken:

"Before the cock crows you will deny me three
times."
He went out and began to weep bitterly.

The Gospel of the Lord.

---

187. Mk 12:28-34

The first of all the commandments.

✠ A reading from the holy Gospel
according to Mark

One of the scribes came to Jesus and asked him,
"Which is the first of all the commandments?"
Jesus replied, "The first is this:
Hear, O Israel!
The Lord our God is Lord alone!
You shall love the Lord your God with all your heart,
with all your soul,
with all your mind,
and with all your strength.
The second is this:
You shall love your neighbor as yourself.
There is no other commandment greater than these."
The scribe said to him, "Well said, teacher.
You are right in saying,
He is One and there is no other than he.
And *to love him with all your heart,*
with all your understanding,
with all your strength,
and to love your neighbor as yourself
is worth more than all burnt offerings and sacrifices."
And when Jesus saw that he answered with understanding,
he said to him,
"You are not far from the Kingdom of God."

And no one dared to ask him any more questions.
The Gospel of the Lord.

---

188. Lk 7:36-50

But the one to whom little is forgiven, loves little.

✠ A reading from the holy Gospel according to Luke

A certain Pharisee invited Jesus to dine with him,
and he entered the Pharisee's house and reclined at table.
Now there was a sinful woman in the city
who learned that he was at table in the house of the Pharisee.
Bringing an alabaster flask of ointment,
she stood behind him at his feet weeping
and began to bathe his feet with her tears.
Then she wiped them with her hair,
kissed them, and anointed them with the ointment.
When the Pharisee who had invited him saw this he said to himself,
"If this man were a prophet,
he would know who and what sort of woman this is who is touching him,
that she is a sinner."
Jesus said to him in reply,
"Simon, I have something to say to you."
"Tell me, teacher," he said.
"Two people were in debt to a certain creditor;
one owed five hundred days' wages and the other owed fifty.
Since they were unable to repay the debt, he forgave it for both.
Which of them will love him more?"
Simon said in reply,

"The one, I suppose, whose larger debt was forgiven."
He said to him, "You have judged rightly."
Then he turned to the woman and said to Simon,
"Do you see this woman?
When I entered your house, you did not give me water for my feet,
but she has bathed them with her tears
and wiped them with her hair.
You did not give me a kiss,
but she has not ceased kissing my feet since the time I entered.
You did not anoint my head with oil,
but she anointed my feet with ointment.
So I tell you, her many sins have been forgiven;
hence, she has shown great love.
But the one to whom little is forgiven, loves little."
He said to her, "Your sins are forgiven."
The others at table said to themselves,
"Who is this who even forgives sins?"
But he said to the woman,
"Your faith has saved you; go in peace."

The Gospel of the Lord.

---

189. Lk 13:1-5

If you do not repent, you will all perish as they did!

✠ A reading from the holy Gospel according to Luke

Some people told Jesus about the Galileans
whose blood Pilate had mingled with the blood of their sacrifices.
He said to them in reply,
"Do you think that because these Galileans suffered in this way
they were greater sinners than all other Galileans?

By no means!
But I tell you, if you do not repent,
you will all perish as they did!
Or those eighteen people who were killed
when the tower at Siloam fell on them—
do you think they were more guilty
than everyone else who lived in Jerusalem?
By no means!
But I tell you, if you do not repent,
you will all perish as they did!"

The Gospel of the Lord.

---

190. Lk 15:1-10

There will be more joy in heaven over one sinner who repents.

✠ A reading from the holy Gospel according to Luke

Tax collectors and sinners were all drawing near to listen to Jesus,
but the Pharisees and scribes began to complain, saying,
"This man welcomes sinners and eats with them."
So to them Jesus addressed this parable.
"What man among you having a hundred sheep and losing one of them
would not leave the ninety-nine in the desert
and go after the lost one until he finds it?
And when he does find it,
he sets it on his shoulders with great joy
and, upon his arrival home,
he calls together his friends and neighbors and says to them,
'Rejoice with me because I have found my lost sheep.'

I tell you, in just the same way
there will be more joy in heaven over one sinner who repents
than over ninety-nine righteous people
who have no need of repentance.

"Or what woman having ten coins and losing one
would not light a lamp and sweep the house,
searching carefully until she finds it?
And when she does find it,
she calls together her friends and neighbors
and says to them,
'Rejoice with me because I have found the coin that I lost.'
In just the same way, I tell you,
there will be rejoicing among the angels of God
over one sinner who repents."

The Gospel of the Lord.

---

191. Lk 15:11-32

While he was still a long way off, his father caught sight of him, and was filled with compassion.

✠ A reading from the holy Gospel according to Luke

Jesus addressed this parable to them.
"A man had two sons, and the younger son said to his father,
'Father, give me the share of your estate that should come to me.'
So the father divided the property between them.
After a few days, the younger son collected all his belongings
and set off to a distant country
where he squandered his inheritance on a life of dissipation.

When he had freely spent everything,
a severe famine struck that country,
and he found himself in dire need.
So he hired himself out to one of the local citizens
who sent him to his farm to tend the swine.
And he longed to eat his fill of the pods on which the swine fed,
but nobody gave him any.
Coming to his senses he thought,
'How many of my father's hired workers
have more than enough food to eat,
but here am I, dying from hunger.
I shall get up and go to my father and I shall say to him,
"Father, I have sinned against heaven and against you.
I no longer deserve to be called your son;
treat me as you would treat one of your hired workers." '
So he got up and went back to his father.
While he was still a long way off,
his father caught sight of him, and was filled with compassion.
He ran to his son, embraced him and kissed him.
His son said to him,
'Father, I have sinned against heaven and against you;
I no longer deserve to be called your son.'
But his father ordered his servants,
'Quickly, bring the finest robe and put it on him;
put a ring on his finger and sandals on his feet.
Take the fattened calf and slaughter it.
Then let us celebrate with a feast,
because this son of mine was dead, and has come to life again;
he was lost, and has been found.'

Then the celebration began.
Now the older son had been out in the field
and, on his way back, as he neared the house,
he heard the sound of music and dancing.
He called one of the servants and asked what this might mean.
The servant said to him,
'Your brother has returned
and your father has slaughtered the fattened calf
because he has him back safe and sound.'
He became angry,
and when he refused to enter the house,
his father came out and pleaded with him.
He said to his father in reply,
'Look, all these years I served you
and not once did I disobey your orders;
yet you never gave me even a young goat to feast on with my friends.
But when your son returns
who swallowed up your property with prostitutes,
for him you slaughter the fattened calf.'
He said to him,
'My son, you are here with me always;
everything I have is yours.
But now we must celebrate and rejoice,
because your brother was dead and has come to life again;
he was lost and has been found.' "

The Gospel of the Lord.

192. Lk 17:1-4

If your brother wrongs you seven times in one day and returns to you seven times saying, "I am sorry," you should forgive him.

✠ **A reading from the holy Gospel according to Luke**

Jesus said to his disciples,
"Things that cause sin will inevitably occur,
but woe to the one through whom they occur.
It would be better for him if a millstone were put around his neck
and he be thrown into the sea
than for him to cause one of these little ones to sin.
Be on your guard!
If your brother sins, rebuke him;
and if he repents, forgive him.
And if he wrongs you seven times in one day
and returns to you seven times saying, 'I am sorry,'
you should forgive him."

The Gospel of the Lord.

---

193. Lk 18:9-14

O God, be merciful to me a sinner.

✠ **A reading from the holy Gospel according to Luke**

Jesus addressed this parable
to those who were convinced of their own righteousness
and despised everyone else.
"Two people went up to the temple area to pray;
one was a Pharisee and the other was a tax collector.

The Pharisee took up his position and spoke this prayer to himself,
'O God, I thank you that I am not like the rest of humanity—
greedy, dishonest, adulterous—or even like this tax collector.
I fast twice a week,
and I pay tithes on my whole income.'
But the tax collector stood off at a distance
and would not even raise his eyes to heaven
but beat his breast and prayed,
'O God, be merciful to me a sinner.'
I tell you, the latter went home justified, not the former;
for everyone who exalts himself will be humbled,
and the one who humbles himself will be exalted."

The Gospel of the Lord.

---

194. Lk 19:1-10

The Son of Man has come to seek and to save what was lost.

✠ A reading from the holy Gospel according to Luke

At that time Jesus came to Jericho and intended to pass through the town.
Now a man there named Zacchaeus,
who was a chief tax collector and also a wealthy man,
was seeking to see who Jesus was;
but he could not see him because of the crowd,
for he was short in stature.
So he ran ahead and climbed a sycamore tree in order to see Jesus,
who was about to pass that way.

When he reached the place, Jesus looked up and said,
"Zacchaeus, come down quickly,
for today I must stay at your house."
And he came down quickly and received him with joy.
When they saw this, they began to grumble, saying,
"He has gone to stay at the house of a sinner."
But Zacchaeus stood there and said to the Lord,
"Behold, half of my possessions, Lord, I shall give to the poor,
and if I have extorted anything from anyone
I shall repay it four times over."
And Jesus said to him,
"Today salvation has come to this house
because this man too is a descendant of Abraham.
For the Son of Man has come to seek
and to save what was lost."

The Gospel of the Lord.

---

195. Lk 23:39-43

Today you will be with me in Paradise.

✠ A reading from the holy Gospel according to Luke

One of the criminals hanging in crucifixion
reviled Jesus, saying,
"Are you not the Christ?
Save yourself and us."
The other man however, rebuking him, said in reply,
"Have you no fear of God,
for you are subject to the same condemnation?
And indeed, we have been condemned justly,
for the sentence we received corresponds to our crimes,
but he has done nothing criminal."

Then he said,
"Jesus, remember me when you come into your Kingdom."
He replied to him,
"Amen, I say to you,
today you will be with me in Paradise."

The Gospel of the Lord.

---

196. Jn 8:1-11

Go, and from now on do not sin any more.

✠ A reading from the holy Gospel according to John

Jesus went to the Mount of Olives.
But early in the morning he arrived again in the temple area,
and all the people started coming to him,
and he sat down and taught them.
Then the scribes and the Pharisees brought a woman
who had been caught in adultery
and made her stand in the middle.
They said to him,
"Teacher, this woman was caught
in the very act of committing adultery.
Now in the law, Moses commanded us to stone such women.
So what do you say?"
They said this to test him,
so that they could have some charge to bring against him.
Jesus bent down and began to write on the ground with his finger.
But when they continued asking him,
he straightened up and said to them,
"Let the one among you who is without sin
be the first to throw a stone at her."

Again he bent down and wrote on the ground.
And in response, they went away one by one,
beginning with the elders.
So he was left alone with the woman before him.
Then Jesus straightened up and said to her,
"Woman, where are they?
Has no one condemned you?"
She replied, "No one, sir."
Then Jesus said, "Neither do I condemn you.
Go, and from now on do not sin any more."

The Gospel of the Lord.

---

197. Jn 8:31-36

Everyone who commits sin is a slave of sin.

✠ A reading from the holy Gospel
according to John

Jesus said to those Jews who believed in him,
"If you remain in my word, you will truly be my disciples,
and you will know the truth, and the truth will set you free."
They answered him, "We are descendants of Abraham
and have never been enslaved to anyone.
How can you say, 'You will become free'?"
Jesus answered them, "Amen, amen, I say to you,
everyone who commits sin is a slave of sin.
A slave does not remain in a household forever,
but a son always remains.
So if the Son frees you, then you will truly be free."

The Gospel of the Lord.

---

198. Jn 15:1-8

He takes away every branch in me that does not bear fruit, and everyone that does he prunes so that it bears more fruit.

✠ A reading from the holy Gospel according to John

Jesus said to his disciples:
"I am the true vine, and my Father is the vine grower.
He takes away every branch in me that does not bear fruit,
and everyone that does he prunes so that it bears more fruit.
You are already pruned because of the word that I spoke to you.
Remain in me, as I remain in you.
Just as a branch cannot bear fruit on its own
unless it remains on the vine,
so neither can you unless you remain in me.
I am the vine, you are the branches.
Whoever remains in me and I in him will bear much fruit,
because without me you can do nothing.
Anyone who does not remain in me
will be thrown out like a branch and wither;
people will gather them and throw them into a fire
and they will be burned.
If you remain in me and my words remain in you,
ask for whatever you want and it will be done for you.
By this is my Father glorified,
that you bear much fruit and become my disciples."

The Gospel of the Lord.

199. Jn 15:9-14

You are my friends if you do what I command you.

✠ A reading from the holy Gospel according to John

Jesus said to his disciples:
"As the Father loves me, so I also love you.
Remain in my love.
If you keep my commandments, you will remain in my love,
just as I have kept my Father's commandments
and remain in his love.

"I have told you this so that my joy might be in you
and your joy might be complete.
This is my commandment: love one another as I love you.
No one has greater love than this,
to lay down one's life for one's friends.
You are my friends if you do what I command you."

The Gospel of the Lord.

---

200. Jn 19:13-37

They will look upon him whom they have pierced.

✠ A reading from the holy Gospel according to John

When Pilate heard these words he brought Jesus out
and seated him on the judge's bench
in the place called Stone Pavement, in Hebrew, Gabbatha.
It was preparation day for Passover, and it was about noon.
And he said to the Jews,
"Behold, your king!"

They cried out,
"Take him away, take him away! Crucify him!"
Pilate said to them,
"Shall I crucify your king?"
The chief priests answered,
"We have no king but Caesar."
Then he handed him over to them to be crucified.

So they took Jesus, and, carrying the cross himself,
he went out to what is called the Place of the Skull,
in Hebrew, Golgotha.
There they crucified him, and with him two others,
one on either side, with Jesus in the middle.
Pilate also had an inscription written and put on the cross.
It read,
"Jesus the Nazorean, the King of the Jews."
Now many of the Jews read this inscription,
because the place where Jesus was crucified was near the city;
and it was written in Hebrew, Latin, and Greek.
So the chief priests of the Jews said to Pilate,
"Do not write 'The King of the Jews,'
but that he said, 'I am the King of the Jews.' "
Pilate answered,
"What I have written, I have written."

When the soldiers had crucified Jesus,
they took his clothes and divided them into four shares,
a share for each soldier.
They also took his tunic, but the tunic was seamless,
woven in one piece from the top down.
So they said to one another,
"Let's not tear it, but cast lots for it to see whose it will be,"

in order that the passage of Scripture might be fulfilled that says:
They divided my garments among them,
and for my vesture they cast lots.
This is what the soldiers did.
Standing by the cross of Jesus were his mother
and his mother's sister, Mary the wife of Clopas,
and Mary Magdalene.
When Jesus saw his mother and the disciple there whom he loved
he said to his mother, "Woman, behold, your son."
Then he said to the disciple,
"Behold, your mother."
And from that hour the disciple took her into his home.

After this, aware that everything was now finished,
in order that the Scripture might be fulfilled,
Jesus said, "I thirst."
There was a vessel filled with common wine.
So they put a sponge soaked in wine on a sprig of hyssop
and put it up to his mouth.
When Jesus had taken the wine, he said,
"It is finished."
And bowing his head, he handed over the spirit.

Now since it was preparation day,
in order that the bodies might not remain on the cross on the sabbath,
for the sabbath day of that week was a solemn one,
the Jews asked Pilate that their legs be broken
and that they be taken down.
So the soldiers came and broke the legs of the first
and then of the other one who was crucified with Jesus.
But when they came to Jesus and saw that he was already dead,
they did not break his legs,

but one soldier thrust his lance into his side,
and immediately Blood and water flowed out.
An eyewitness has testified, and his testimony is true;
he knows that he is speaking the truth,
so that you also may come to believe.
For this happened so that the Scripture passage might be fulfilled:
Not a bone of it will be broken.
And again another passage says:
They will look upon him whom they have pierced.

The Gospel of the Lord.

---

201. Jn 20:19-23

Receive the Holy Spirit. Whose sins you forgive are forgiven them.

✠ A reading from the holy Gospel according to John

On the evening of that first day of the week,
when the doors were locked, where the disciples were,
for fear of the Jews,
Jesus came and stood in their midst
and said to them, "Peace be with you."
When he had said this, he showed them his hands and his side.
The disciples rejoiced when they saw the Lord.
Jesus said to them again, "Peace be with you.
As the Father has sent me, so I send you."
And when he had said this, he breathed on them and said to them,
"Receive the Holy Spirit.
Whose sins you forgive are forgiven them,
and whose sins you retain are retained."

The Gospel of the Lord.

Invitation of the Minister for the General Confession of Sins

202. If the prayer is directed to the Father:

Dear friends,
so that, we who lament our past sins,
may not experience future ills
nor commit further actions we would regret,
let us humbly pray
to the almighty and merciful God,
who desires not the death of sinners
but rather that they turn back and live.

℟. Spare us, Lord; spare your people.

2

According to the multitude of his mercies,
our compassionate God
blots out sins by our repentance
and removes past faults by his pardon.
Let us pray with confidence
that in his kindness
he may hear those who seek forgiveness
of all their sins
through a full and heartfelt confession.

℟. Lord, we ask you, hear our prayer.

3

God handed over his Son
for our transgressions
and raised him up for our justification.
Let us humbly pray to him, as we say:

℟. Have mercy on your people, Lord.

4

Let us pray to God our Father,
who awaits the return
of the children estranged from him
and embraces them when they repent,
that he will lovingly welcome those
who come back to his house.

℟. We have sinned, O Lord;
look not on our sins.

Or:

℟. Father, we have sinned against you,
and no longer deserve
to be called your children.

5

Let us pray to our God,
who seeks out the lost,
brings back the abandoned,
binds up the broken,
and strengthens the weak.

℟. Lord, heal our infirmities.

203. If the prayer is directed to Christ:

1

In humble prayer
let us call upon Jesus Christ,
the victor over sin and death,
that by his mercy we may receive
both pardon for offenses against God
and reconciliation with the Church,
whom we have wounded by our sins.

℟. Lord Jesus, save us.

2

With confident prayer and firm hope
let us draw near to Christ,
who out of immense love
entered willingly into his Passion and Death
for our sins and those of all people,
that he might obtain salvation for all.

℟. Christ, hear us.

3

Let us pray with confidence to Christ,
the Good Shepherd,
who seeks out the lost sheep
and, when he has found it,
carries it home rejoicing.

℟. Lord, seek us out and bring us home.

4

Brothers and sisters,
in humility and trust
let us offer our prayers to Christ,
who bore our sins in his own body
on the tree,
so that, dead to sin,
we may live for righteousness,
for by his wounds we have been healed.
Let us therefore say together:

℟. Lord, to whom shall we go?
You have the words of eternal life.
And we have come to believe and know
that you are the Christ, the Son of God.

Or:

℟. In your mercy, help us.

5

Let us pray with confidence
to Christ the Lord,
who was handed over for our transgressions
and rose again for our justification,
as we say:

℟. You are our Savior.

Or:

℟. Christ, Son of the living God,
have mercy on us.

Penitential Invocations

(At least one of the invocations should always be a petition for a true conversion of heart.)

204. If the prayer is addressed to the Father:

—That you will grant us frail sinners,
who have marred the integrity
of the Church,
full remission of our sins
and restore us to full communion
with our brothers and sisters.

℟. Lord, we ask you, hear our prayer.

Or:

℟. Lord, have mercy on us.

Or another suitable response may be used.

—That you will admit us to
the Sacrament of Reconciliation,
for we have no confidence
except in your mercy.—℟.

—That, with a sincere heart,
we may strive for our own conversion
and that of our brothers and sisters
by our charity, example, and prayers.—℟.

—That, as we confess our sins today,
you will rescue us from slavery to sin
and lead us to the freedom
of your children.—℟.

—That, reconciled with you
and with one another,
we may be made a living sign
of your love in the world.—℟.

—That through
the Sacrament of Reconciliation
we may receive more fully
your peace within ourselves
and pursue it more effectively
in the world.—℟.

—That through this sign of your love,
by which you forgive our sins,
we may learn to love
our brothers and sisters
and to forgive them their trespasses.—℟.

—That we, who beseech your mercy,
may come to your table
with the wedding garment
we have received.—℟.

—That, with our sins forgiven,
you will lead us in the paths
of justice and love
and bring us to the rewards
of eternal peace.—℟.

—That by your light
you will dispel our darkness
and lead us in the way of truth.—℟.

—That we, who suffer justly for our sins,
may, in your mercy, be set free
for the glory of your name.—℟.

—That by your power you will keep safe
from all adversity
those you loose from the bonds of sin
by your loving kindness.—℟.

—That, looking upon our frailty,
you will not in anger reprove us
for our wickedness
but in your boundless mercy
will purify, refine, and save us.—℟.

—That your mercy will strip us
of all our old ways
and make us capable
of new ways of holiness.—℟.

—That we, who have strayed from you,
may return to the way
of justice, love, and peace.—℟.

—That your redeeming mercy
will overcome
all the ruin brought about
by our wickedness.—℟.

—That you will blot out our past sins
and prepare us for the life to come.—℟.

2

The following invocations may be used with a variable response or with an invariable response as in *The Liturgy of the Hours.*

—In your kindness,
forgive the sins we have committed
against the unity of your family

℟. and grant us to be
of one heart and one mind.

—We have sinned, O Lord, we have sinned;

℟. blot out our offenses
by your saving grace.

—Grant that we sinners
may obtain your pardon

℟. and be reconciled also with your Church.

—Grant us to cherish your friendship
more and more
through sincere conversion

℟. and to atone for our offenses
against your wisdom and goodness.

—Purify and renew your Church, O Lord,

℟. that she may bear
ever greater witness to you.

—Inspire all who have separated
themselves from you
because of sins and scandals,

℟. that they may return to you
and remain in your love.

—Grant that we may carry in our bodies the Death of your Son,

℟. for in his Body
you have brought us to life.

—Graciously hear the prayers of those who call upon you,
we ask, O Lord,
and forgive the sins of those who confess to you,

℟. granting us in your kindness
both pardon and peace.

—We have greatly sinned, O Lord,
but we profess your mercy;

℟. convert us, and we shall be converted.

—May we be received with a humble heart and a contrite spirit,

℟. for those who trust in you
will not be put to shame.

—We have sinned and done evil, departing from you,

℟. and have offended in all things
and have not kept your laws.

—Turn, O Lord, and have mercy on us,
take away our iniquities,

℟. and cast all our sins
into the depths of the sea.

—Grant that, made righteous,
we may exult in you, O Lord,

℟. and glory in uprightness of heart.

205. If the prayer is addressed to Christ:

—By your Death you reconciled us
to the Father and saved us. (Romans 5:10)

℟. Lord, have mercy on us.

Or:

℟. Christ, graciously hear us.

Or another suitable response may be used.

—You died and rose again
and are seated at the right hand of the Father
to intercede for us.—℟. (Romans 8:34)

—You became for us wisdom from God,
our righteousness, sanctification,
and redemption.—℟. (1 Corinthians 1:30)

—You have washed, sanctified,
and justified all people
in the Spirit of our God.—℟. (1 Corinthians 6:11)

—You have said that if we sin against
our brothers and sisters
we sin against you.—℟. (1 Corinthians 8:12)

—Though you were rich,
you were made poor for us,
so that by your poverty
we might be made rich.—℟. (2 Corinthians 8:9)

—You gave yourself for our sins,
that you might deliver us
from the evil of this world.—℟. (Galatians 1:4)

—You rose from the dead
and rescued us from the wrath to come.—℟.
(1 Thessalonians 1:10)

—You came into this world
to save sinners.—℟. (1 Timothy 1:15)

—You gave yourself as a ransom for all.—℟.
(1 Timothy 2:6)

—You destroyed death and revealed life.—℟.
(2 Timothy 1:10)

—You will come to judge the living
and the dead.—℟. (2 Timothy 4:1)

—You gave yourself for us,
to redeem us from all iniquity
and to cleanse for yourself
an acceptable people,
pursuing good works.—℟. (Titus 2:14)

—You were made
a merciful and faithful high priest
in the things pertaining to God,
to make expiation for the transgressions
of the people.—℟. (Hebrews 2:17)

—You were made
the source of eternal salvation
for all who obey you.—℟. (Hebrews 5:9)

—Through the Holy Spirit
you offered yourself unblemished to God,
cleansing our consciences
from dead works.—℟. (Hebrews 9:14)

—You were offered up to take away
the sins of many.—℟. (Hebrews 9:28)

—You died once for our sins,
the righteous for the unrighteous.—℟.
(1 Peter 3:18)

—You are the expiation for our sins,
and not for ours alone,
but for those of the whole world.—℟. (1 John 2:2)

—You died,
so that those who believe in you
might not perish,
but have eternal life.—℟. (1 John 3:16, 35)

—You came into this world
to seek out and save what was lost.—℟.
(Matthew 18:11)

—You were sent by the Father
not to judge the world,
but that the world might be saved
through you.—℟. (John 3:17)

—You have power on earth
to forgive sins.—℟. (Mark 2:10)

—You call to yourself
all who labor and are burdened,
that you may refresh them.—℟. (Matthew 11:28)

—You gave to your Apostles
the keys of the Kingdom of Heaven,
that they might bind and loose.—℟.
(Matthew 16:19; 18:18)

—You summed up the whole law
in the love of God and neighbor.—℟.
(Matthew 22:38-40)

—Jesus, the life of all,
who came into the world,
that we might have life
and have it more abundantly.—℟. (John 10:10)

—Jesus, Good Shepherd,
who laid down your life for the sheep.—℟.
(John 10:11)

—Jesus, unshakeable truth,
who have set us free.—℟. (John 14:6; 8:32, 36)

—Jesus, the only way,
through which all must come
to the Father.—℟. (John 14:6)

—Jesus, the Resurrection and the Life,
through whom those who believe in you,
even though they die, shall live.—℟. (John 11:25)

—Jesus, the true vine,
whose fruit-bearing branches
the Father will prune,
that they may bear more fruit.—℟. (John 15:1-2)

2

The following invocations may be used with a variable response or with an invariable response as in *The Liturgy of the Hours.*

—Physician of body and soul,
heal the wounds of our hearts,

℟. that we may receive
the continual protection of holiness.

—Grant us to strip off
the old self with its actions

℟. and be clothed with you, the New Man.

—Our Redeemer,
grant us to cling more firmly to your Passion
through penance,

℟. that we may attain more fully the glory
of the resurrection.

—May your Mother, the refuge of sinners,
intercede for us,

℟. that in your kindness
you will pardon our sins.

—You forgave the sins
of the penitent woman;

℟. do not withhold your mercy from us.

—You placed the wandering sheep
on your shoulders;

℟. have pity on us and lift us up.

**—You offered paradise
to the thief crucified with you;**

℟. bring us with you into your Kingdom.

—You died for us and rose again;

℟. make us sharers in your Death
and Resurrection.

PROCLAMATION OF PRAISE

206.

1 Psalm 32 (31):1-2, 3-4, 5, 6, 7, 10-11

℟. (11a) Rejoice in the Lord, exult you just!

**Blessed is he whose transgression is forgiven,
whose sin is remitted.
Blessed the man to whom the LORD imputes
no guilt,
in whose spirit is no guile.**—℟.

**I kept it secret and my frame was wasted.
I groaned all day long,
For your hand, by day and by night,
lay heavy upon me.
Indeed, my strength was dried up
as by the summer's heat.**—℟.

**To you I have acknowledged my sin;
my guilt I did not hide.
I said, "I will confess my transgression to the
LORD."
And you have forgiven the guilt of my
sin.**—℟.

So let each faithful one pray to you
in the time of need.
The floods of water may reach high,
but such a one they shall not reach.—℟.

You are a hiding place for me;
you keep me safe from distress;
you surround me with cries of deliverance.
—℟.

Many sorrows has the wicked,
but loving mercy surrounds the one who trusts in the LORD.
Rejoice in the LORD, exult you just!
Ring out your joy, all you upright of heart!—℟.

2 Psalm 98 (97):1, 2-3b, 3c-4, 5-6, 7-9b, 9cd

℟. (3a) The Lord has remembered his merciful love.

O sing a new song to the LORD,
for he has worked wonders.
His right hand and his holy arm
have brought salvation.—℟.

The LORD has made known his salvation,
has shown his deliverance to the nations.
He has remembered his merciful love
and his truth for the house of Israel.—℟.

All the ends of the earth have seen
  the salvation of our God.
Shout to the LORD, all the earth;
  break forth into joyous song,
  and sing out your praise.—℟.

Sing psalms to the LORD with the harp,
  with the harp and the sound of song.
With trumpets and the sound of the horn,
  raise a shout before the King, the LORD.
    —℟.

Let the sea and all within it thunder;
  the world, and those who dwell in it.
Let the rivers clap their hands,
  and the hills ring out their joy
at the presence of the LORD, for he comes,
  he comes to judge the earth.—℟.

He will judge the world with justice,
  and the peoples with faithfulness.—℟.

3

Psalm 100 (99):1b-2, 3, 4, 5

℟. (5ab) How good is the Lord, eternal his merciful love.

Cry out with joy to the LORD, all the earth.
  Serve the LORD with gladness.
  Come before him, singing for joy.—℟.

Know that he, the LORD, is God.
  He made us; we belong to him.
  We are his people, the sheep of his flock.
    —℟.

Enter his gates with thanksgiving
and his courts with songs of praise.
Give thanks to him, and bless his name.
—℟.

Indeed, how good is the LORD,
eternal his merciful love.
He is faithful from age to age.—℟.

4 Psalm 119 (118):1 and 10, 11-12, 13 and 15, 16 and 18, 33 and 105, 169-170, 174-175

℟. (12) Blest are you, O Lord; teach me your statutes.

Blessed are those whose way is blameless,
who walk in the law of the LORD!
I seek you with all my heart;
let me not stray from your commands.—℟.

I treasure your word in my heart,
lest I sin against you.
Blest are you, O LORD;
teach me your statutes.—℟.

With my lips have I recounted
all the decrees of your mouth.
I will ponder your precepts,
and consider your paths.—℟.

I take delight in your statutes;
I will not forget your word.
Open my eyes, that I may see
the wonders of your law.—℟.

LORD, teach me the way of your statutes,
and I will keep them to the end.
Your word is a lamp for my feet,
and a light for my path.—℟.

Let my cry come before you, O LORD;
give me insight by your word.
Let my pleading come before you;
rescue me according to your promise.—℟.

I long for your salvation, O LORD,
and your law is my delight.
My soul shall live and praise you.
Your judgments give me help.—℟.

5 Psalm 103 (102):1-2, 3-4, 8-10, 11-12, 13-14, 15-16, 17-18

℟. (17ab) The mercy of the Lord is everlasting upon those who hold him in fear.

Bless the LORD, O my soul,
and all within me, his holy name.
Bless the LORD, O my soul,
and never forget all his benefits.—℟.

It is the Lord who forgives all your sins,
who heals every one of your ills,
who redeems your life from the grave,
who crowns you with mercy and compassion.—℟.

The LORD is compassionate and gracious,
slow to anger and rich in mercy.
He will not always find fault;
nor persist in his anger forever.

He does not treat us according to our sins,
nor repay us according to our faults.—℟.

For as the heavens are high above the earth,
so strong his mercy for those who fear him.
As far as the east is from the west,
so far from us does he remove our trans-gressions.—℟.

As a father has compassion on his children,
the LORD's compassion is on those who fear him.
For he knows of what we are made;
he remembers that we are dust.—℟.

Man, his days are like grass;
he flowers like the flower of the field.
The wind blows, and it is no more,
and its place never sees it again.—℟.

But the mercy of the LORD is everlasting
upon those who hold him in fear,
upon children's children his justice,
for those who keep his covenant,
and remember to fulfill his commands.—℟.

6 Psalm 145 (144):1, 2-3, 4-5, 6-7, 8-9, 10-11, 12-13b, 13c-14, 15-16, 17-18, 19-20, 21

℟. (5) I will bless you day after day, O Lord,
and praise your name forever.

I will extol you, my God and king,
and bless your name forever and ever.—℟.

I will bless you day after day,
and praise your name forever and ever.
The LORD is great and highly to be praised;
his greatness cannot be measured.—℟.

Age to age shall proclaim your works,
shall declare your mighty deeds.
They will tell of your great glory and splendor,
and recount your wonderful works.—℟.

They will speak of your awesome deeds,
recount your greatness and might.
They will recall your abundant goodness,
and sing of your righteous deeds with joy.—℟.

The LORD is kind and full of compassion,
slow to anger, abounding in mercy.
How good is the LORD to all,
compassionate to all his creatures.—℟.

All your works shall thank you, O LORD,
and all your faithful ones bless you.
They shall speak of the glory of your reign,
and declare your mighty deeds.—℟.

They shall make known your might to the whole human race,
and the glorious splendor of your reign.
Your kingdom is an everlasting kingdom;
your rule endures for all generations.—℟.

The LORD is faithful in all his words,
and holy in all his deeds.
The LORD supports all who fall,
and raises up all who are bowed down.
—℟.

The eyes of all look to you,
and you give them their food in due season.
You open your hand and satisfy
the desire of every living thing.—℟.

The LORD is just in all his ways,
and holy in all his deeds.
The LORD is close to all who call him,
who call on him in truth.—℟.

He fulfills the desires of those who fear him;
he hears their cry and he saves them.
The LORD keeps watch over all who love him;
the wicked he will utterly destroy.—℟.

Let my mouth speak the praise of the LORD;
let all flesh bless his holy name
forever, for ages unending.—℟.

7 Psalm 146 (145):1b-2, 3-4, 5-7a, 7b-8b, 8c-10

℟. (2b) I will sing praise to my God while I live.

My soul, give praise to the LORD;
I will praise the LORD all my life,
sing praise to my God while I live.—℟.

Put no trust in princes,
  or anyone who cannot save.
Take their breath, they return to the earth,
  and their plans that day come to nothing.
    —℟.

Blessed is he who is helped by Jacob's God,
  whose hope is in the LORD his God,
who made the heavens and the earth,
  the seas and all they contain,
who preserves fidelity forever,
  who does justice to those who are oppressed.—℟.

It is he who gives bread to the hungry,
  the LORD who sets prisoners free,
the LORD who opens the eyes of the blind,
  the LORD who raises up those who are bowed down.—℟.

It is the LORD who loves the just,
  the LORD who protects the stranger
and upholds the orphan and the widow,
  but thwarts the path of the wicked.
The LORD will reign forever,
  your God, O Zion, from age to age.—℟.

8

Isaiah 12:1bcd, 2, 3, 4, 5-6

℟. (4b) Give thanks to the Lord, invoke his name.

I give thanks to you, O LORD!
  For though you were angry with me,

your anger turned back, and you consoled
me.—℟.

Behold, God is my salvation!
I will trust and will not be afraid,
for the LORD is my strength and my praise,
and he has been my salvation.—℟.

With joy will you draw water
from the springs of salvation.—℟.

And you will say on that day:
Give thanks to the LORD, invoke his name;
make known among the peoples his deeds;
proclaim that his name is exalted.—℟.

Sing to the LORD for he has wrought wonders;
let this be known through all the earth.
Shout aloud and sing praise, you who dwell
in Zion,
for great in your midst is the Holy One of
Israel.—℟.

9 Isaiah 61:10, 11

℟. (10b) My soul shall exult in my God.

I will greatly rejoice in the LORD,
and my soul shall exult in my God;
for he has clothed me in the garments of
salvation,
and wrapped me in the robe of saving justice,
like a bridegroom adorned with a crown,
and like a bride bedecked with her
jewels.—℟.

For as the earth brings forth its growth,
and a garden makes what is sown in it sprout up,
so the Lord God will make righteousness and praise
sprout up in the sight of all the nations.
—℟.

10

Jeremiah 31:10-11, 12, 13-14

℟. (cf. 11a) The Lord has ransomed his people.

Hear the word of the Lord, O nations;
declare it to the distant isles and say,
"He who scattered Israel will gather him
and guard him as a shepherd his flock."
For the Lord has ransomed Jacob,
redeemed him from a hand too strong for him.—℟.

They shall come and sing praise on the heights of Zion,
come streaming to the bounty of the Lord—
to the grain and the wine and the oil,
to the yearlings of the flock and the herd.
Their soul shall be like a watered garden,
and they shall languish no more.—℟.

Then the maiden shall rejoice in a dance,
the young men and old together.
"I will change their mourning into joy;

I will console them, giving gladness for sorrow.
I will fill with rich fare the soul of my priests,
and my people shall be filled with my bounty."—℟.

11 Daniel 3:52ab, 52cd, 53, 54, 55, 56, 57

℟. (57) Bless the Lord, all you works of the Lord, praise and highly exalt him forever.

VT

Blessed are you, O LORD, the God of our ancestors,
to be praised and highly exalted forever. —℟.

Blessed is your glorious and holy name,
to be highly praised and exalted forever. —℟.

Blessed are you in the temple of your holy glory,
to be highly praised and glorified forever.—℟.

Blessed are you on the throne of your kingdom,
to be praised and highly exalted forever. —℟.

Blessed are you who look into the depths,
seated upon the cherubim,
to be praised and highly exalted forever. —℟.

Blessed are you in the firmament of heaven,
worthy of praise and highly exalted forever.—℟.

Bless the Lord, all you works of the Lord,
praise and highly exalt him forever.—℟.

12 Luke 1:46-48, 49-50, 51-53, 54-55

℟. (54b) The Lord is mindful of his mercy.

My soul proclaims the greatness of the Lord,
and my spirit rejoices in God my Savior,
for he has looked upon his handmaid in her lowliness;
for behold, from this day forward,
all generations will call me blessed.—℟.

For the Almighty has done great things for me,
and holy is his name.
His mercy is from age to age
for those who fear him.—℟.

He has made known the strength of his arm,
and has scattered the proud in their conceit of heart.
He has cast down the mighty from their thrones
and has exalted those who are lowly.
He has filled the hungry with good things,
and has sent the rich away empty.—℟.

He has helped his servant Israel,
mindful of his mercy,

even as he promised to our fathers,
to Abraham and his descendants forever.
—℟.

13 Ephesians 1:3-4, 5-6, 7-8, 9-10

℟. (cf. 3a, 4a) Blessed be God who has chosen us in Christ.

Blessed be the God and Father of our Lord Jesus Christ,
who has blessed us in Christ
with every spiritual blessing in the heavens;
just as he has chosen us in him
before the foundation of the world
to be holy and blameless before him in love.—℟.

He destined us for adoption
to himself through Jesus Christ,
in accord with the good pleasure of his will,
to the praise of his glorious grace,
with which he favored us in the Beloved.
—℟.

In him we have redemption through his blood,
the forgiveness of transgressions,
in accord with the riches of his grace
lavished on us in all wisdom and insight.
—℟.

He has made known to us the mystery of his will
in accord with his good pleasure,
which he set forth in Christ as a plan,
a plan for the fullness of times,
to recapitulate all things in him,
things in heaven, and things on earth.—℟.

14

Revelation 15:3, 4ab, 4cdef

℟. (3ab) Great and wondrous are your works, O Lord!

Great and wondrous are your works,
O Lord, Almighty God!
Just and true are your ways,
O King of the nations!—℟.

Who would not fear, O Lord,
and glorify your name?—℟.

For you alone are the Holy One,
for all nations will come,
and they will worship before you,
for your righteous deeds have been revealed.—℟.

Concluding Prayer

207.

It is right and just
always and everywhere to give you thanks,
almighty and eternal God,
who justly chastise and lovingly pardon,
at all times showing mercy.

For you govern us by the law
that, in correcting us, you do not allow us
to perish eternally
and, in sparing us, you give us room
for amendment.
Through Christ our Lord.

℟. Amen.

208.

O God, Creator and Ruler of all light,
who so loved this world
that for our salvation you handed over
your Only Begotten Son,
by whose Cross we have been redeemed,
by whose Death we have been brought to life,
by whose Passion we have been saved,
by whose Resurrection we have been glorified,
through him we humbly beseech you:
graciously be with this family of yours
in all things.

May we have a holy fear of you
in our understanding,
faith in our hearts,
justice in our works,
filial devotion in our actions,
truth on our lips,
discipline in our conduct,
and so worthily and rightly receive
the reward of immortality.
Through Christ our Lord.

℟. Amen.

209.

Lord Jesus Christ,
rich in forgiveness,
you willed to take on the lowliness
of the flesh,
so that you might leave us
an example of humility
and make us steadfast in all suffering.
Grant that we may always hold fast
to the good things
we have received from you
and, whenever we fall into sin,
be raised up through penance.
Who live and reign for ever and ever.

℟. Amen.

210.

O God, by whose grace
we sinners are made just
and from our misery made blessed,
stand by your works,
stand by your gifts,
that those justified by faith
may not lack the courage of perseverance.
Through Christ our Lord.

℟. Amen.

211.

O God, our Father,
you have forgiven our sins
and given us your peace;

grant that we may always forgive
each other's offenses
and work together for peace in the world.
Through Christ our Lord.

℟. Amen.

FORMULAS OF BLESSING

212.

And may the blessing of almighty God,
the Father, and the Son, ✠ and the Holy Spirit,
come down on you
and remain with you for ever.

℟. Amen.

213.

May the Father,
who has given us birth to eternal life,
bless us.

℟. Amen.

May the Son,
who died for us and rose again,
grant us salvation.

℟. Amen.

May the Spirit,
who has been poured into our hearts
and has led us back onto the right path,
sanctify us.

℟. Amen.

214.

May the Father,
who has called us to adoption as his children,
bless us.

℟. Amen.

May the Son,
who has accepted us
as his brothers and sisters, come to our aid.

℟. Amen.

May the Spirit,
who has made us his temple, be with us.

℟. Amen.

APPENDIX I

ABSOLUTION FROM CENSURES

1. When a Priest, in accordance with the norm of law, absolves a properly disposed penitent within the sacramental forum from a censure *latæ sententiæ*, the formula of absolution is not to be changed. It is enough that the confessor intend to absolve the properly disposed penitent also from censures. Before absolving from sins, however, the confessor may absolve from the censure, using the formula that is given below for use outside the Sacrament of Penance.

2. When a Priest, in accordance with the norm of law, absolves a penitent from a censure outside the Sacrament of Penance, he uses the following formula: A1

By the power granted to me,
I absolve you
from the bond of excommunication
(or: suspension or: interdict).
In the name of the Father, and of the Son, ✠
and of the Holy Spirit.

The penitent replies:

Amen.

DISPENSATION FROM IRREGULARITY

3. If a penitent is affected by an irregularity, a Priest, in accordance with the norm of law, when he dispenses the penitent from the irregularity, either during confession, after absolution has been given, or apart from the Sacrament of Penance, says:

By the power granted to me,
I dispense you from the irregularity
which you have incurred.
In the name of the Father, and of the Son, ✠
and of the Holy Spirit.

The penitent replies:

Amen.

APPENDIX II

EXAMPLES OF PENITENTIAL CELEBRATIONS

THE PART THAT FOLLOWS HAS BEEN COMPOSED WITH CARE AND DILIGENCE BY THE SACRED CONGREGATION FOR DIVINE WORSHIP TO HELP THOSE WHO PREPARE OR LEAD PENITENTIAL CELEBRATIONS

PREPARING PENITENTIAL CELEBRATIONS

1. Penitential celebrations, mentioned in *The Order of Penance* (nos. 36-37), are very useful for fostering the spirit and virtue of penance in the life of individuals or of communities and also for preparing for a more fruitful celebration of the Sacrament of Penance. Care should be taken that, in the minds of the faithful, these celebrations are not confused with sacramental confession and absolution.[1]

2. Penitential celebrations, especially those designed for various groups and their needs, should carefully take into consideration the special conditions of life, the manner of speaking and the power of comprehension of those who have gathered. The liturgical commissions[2] and individual Christian communities should take care to prepare these celebrations in such a way

[1]Cf. Sacred Congregation for the Doctrine of the Faith, *Pastoral Norms for the Administration of General Sacramental Absolution*, June 16, 1972, no. X: *Acta Apostolicæ Sedis* 64 (1972), p. 513.

[2]Cf. Sacred Congregation of Rites, Instruction *Inter Œcumenici*, Sept. 26, 1964, no. 39: *Acta Apostolicæ Sedis* 56 (1964), p. 110.

that, for each group and for the various circumstances, the most suitable texts are chosen and the most suitable format adopted.

3. To help in this task, various and diverse examples of penitential celebrations are presented here. They should be understood as models and should be adapted to the specific conditions and needs of each community.

4. Sometimes in these celebrations the Sacrament of Penance is included. In this case, after the readings and Homily, the Order for Reconciling Several Penitents with Individual Confession and Absolution (nos. 54-59) is used, or, in special cases permitted by law, the Order for Reconciling Penitents with General Confession and Absolution (nos. 60-63).

I. Penitential Celebrations during Lent

5. Lent is the principal time of penance both for individual Christians and, at the same time, for the whole Church. It is therefore desirable that, during Lent, through penitential celebrations, the Christian community be prepared for a fuller participation in the Paschal Mystery.[1]

6. The penitential character of the Liturgy of the Word in the Masses for Lent should be kept in mind. Texts from the *Lectionary for Mass* and *The Roman Missal* may appropriately be used in penitential celebrations held during Lent.

7. Two examples of penitential celebrations more suitable for Lent are given here. The first emphasizes penance as strengthening or restoring baptismal grace; the second shows penance as a preparation for a fuller participation in the Paschal Mystery of Christ and the Church.

First Example

"Penance leads to a strengthening or restoring of baptismal grace"

8. a) After an appropriate liturgical song and the greeting by the minister, the meaning of this celebration is explained to the people. This prepares the Christian community to recall their baptismal grace at the Easter Vigil and to reach newness of life in Christ through freedom from sins.

[1]Cf. Second Vatican Council, Constitution on the Sacred Liturgy, *Sacrosanctum Concilium*, no. 109; Paul VI, Apostolic Constitution *Pænitemini*, Feb. 17, 1966, no. IX: *Acta Apostolicæ Sedis* 58 (1966), p. 185.

9. b) Prayer

Let us pray, brothers and sisters (brethren),
that we, who through our sins
were unmindful of the grace of Baptism,
may now be restored to that grace
through penance.

Let us kneel (or: Bow your heads before God).

All pray in silence for a while.

Let us stand (or: Raise your heads).

We pray, O Lord,
guard with your unfailing love,
those you have washed clean,
that, redeemed by your Passion,
they may rejoice in your Resurrection.
Who live and reign for ever and ever.

℟. Amen.

10. c) Readings

—Just as the Israelites, after crossing the Red Sea, forgot about the wonders of God, so too the members of the new People of God, after the grace of Baptism, often turn again to sin.

FIRST READING
1 Cor 10:1-13

A reading from the first Letter of Saint Paul to the Corinthians

I do not want you to be unaware, brothers and sisters,
that our ancestors were all under the cloud

and all passed through the sea,
and all of them were baptized into Moses
in the cloud and in the sea.
All ate the same spiritual food,
and all drank the same spiritual drink,
for they drank from a spiritual rock that followed them,
and the rock was the Christ.
Yet God was not pleased with most of them,
for they were struck down in the desert.

These things happened as examples for us,
so that we might not desire evil things, as they did.
And do not become idolaters, as some of them did,
as it is written,
The people sat down to eat and drink,
and rose up to revel.
Let us not indulge in immorality as some of them did,
and twenty-three thousand fell within a single day.
Let us not test Christ as some of them did,
and suffered death by serpents.
Do not grumble as some of them did,
and suffered death by the destroyer.
These things happened to them as an example,
and they have been written down as a warning to us,
upon whom the end of the ages has come.
Therefore, whoever thinks he is standing secure should take care not to fall.
No trial has come to you but what is human.
God is faithful and will not let you be tried beyond your strength;
but with the trial he will also provide a way out,
so that you may be able to bear it.

The word of the Lord.

RESPONSORIAL PSALM

Ps 106 (105):6-7b, 7c-8, 9-10, 13-14, 19-20, 21-22

℟. (6) We have done wrong; our deeds have been evil.

Like our fathers, we have sinned.
We have done wrong; our deeds have been evil.
Our forebears, when they were in Egypt,
did not grasp the meaning of your wonders.—℟.

They forgot the great number of your mercies,
at the Red Sea defied the Most High.
Yet he saved them for the sake of his name,
in order to make known his power.—℟.

He rebuked the Red Sea; it dried up,
and he led them through the deep as through the desert.
He saved them from the hand of the foe;
he freed them from the grip of the enemy.—℟.

But they soon forgot his deeds,
and would not wait upon his counsel.
They yielded to their cravings in the desert,
and put God to the test in the wilderness.—℟.

They fashioned a calf at Horeb
and worshiped an image of metal;
they exchanged their glory
for the image of a bull that eats grass.—℟.

They forgot the God who was their savior,
who had done such great things in Egypt,
such wonders in the land of Ham,
such awesome deeds at the Red Sea.—℟.

—The son who leaves his father and his home is welcomed again with love by his father; the sheep who strays from the flock is sought again with great care by the shepherd. In the same way, God again seeks us who have sinned after the grace of Baptism and accepts us with love when we return to him, while the whole Church rejoices.

GOSPEL

1 Lk 15:4-7

✠ A reading from the holy Gospel according to Luke

Jesus addressed this parable to them:
"What man among you having a hundred sheep and losing one of them
would not leave the ninety-nine in the desert
and go after the lost one until he finds it?
And when he does find it,
he sets it on his shoulders with great joy
and, upon his arrival home,
he calls together his friends and neighbors and says to them,
'Rejoice with me because I have found my lost sheep.'
I tell you, in just the same way
there will be more joy in heaven over one sinner who repents
than over ninety-nine righteous people
who have no need of repentance."

The Gospel of the Lord.

---

2 Lk 15:11-32

✠ A reading from the holy Gospel according to Luke

Jesus addressed this parable to them:
"A man had two sons, and the younger son said to his father,

'Father, give me the share of your estate that should come to me.'
So the father divided the property between them.
After a few days, the younger son collected all his belongings
and set off to a distant country
where he squandered his inheritance on a life of dissipation.
When he had freely spent everything,
a severe famine struck that country,
and he found himself in dire need.
So he hired himself out to one of the local citizens
who sent him to his farm to tend the swine.
And he longed to eat his fill of the pods on which the swine fed,
but nobody gave him any.
Coming to his senses he thought,
'How many of my father's hired workers
have more than enough food to eat,
but here am I, dying from hunger.
I shall get up and go to my father and I shall say to him,
"Father, I have sinned against heaven and against you.
I no longer deserve to be called your son;
treat me as you would treat one of your hired workers." '
So he got up and went back to his father.
While he was still a long way off,
his father caught sight of him, and was filled with compassion.
He ran to his son, embraced him and kissed him.
His son said to him,
'Father, I have sinned against heaven and against you;
I no longer deserve to be called your son.'
But his father ordered his servants,

'Quickly, bring the finest robe and put it on him;
put a ring on his finger and sandals on his feet.
Take the fattened calf and slaughter it.
Then let us celebrate with a feast,
because this son of mine was dead, and has come to life again;
he was lost, and has been found.'
Then the celebration began.
Now the older son had been out in the field
and, on his way back, as he neared the house,
he heard the sound of music and dancing.
He called one of the servants and asked what this might mean.
The servant said to him,
'Your brother has returned
and your father has slaughtered the fattened calf
because he has him back safe and sound.'
He became angry,
and when he refused to enter the house,
his father came out and pleaded with him.
He said to his father in reply,
'Look, all these years I served you
and not once did I disobey your orders;
yet you never gave me even a young goat to feast on with my friends.
But when your son returns
who swallowed up your property with prostitutes,
for him you slaughter the fattened calf.'
He said to him,
'My son, you are here with me always;
everything I have is yours.
But now we must celebrate and rejoice,
because your brother was dead and has come to life again;
he was lost and has been found.' "

The Gospel of the Lord.

11. d) Homily

The Homily may address:

—the need to fulfill the grace of Baptism by living faithfully the Gospel of Christ (cf. 1 Cor 10:1-13);

—the seriousness of sin committed after Baptism (cf. Heb 6:4-8);

—the infinite mercy of our God and Father, who again and again welcomes us who turn back to him after having sinned (cf. Lk 15);

—Easter as the feast when the Church rejoices over the Christian Initiation of Catechumens and the Reconciliation of Penitents.

12. e) Examination of Conscience

After the Homily, the examination of conscience takes place; a sample text is found in Appendix III, p. 348. A period of silence should always be included, so that each person may examine his (her) conscience in a more personal manner. In a special way the people should examine their conscience on the baptismal promises that will be renewed at the Easter Vigil.

13. f) Penitential Act

The Deacon (or another minister, if there is no Deacon) speaks to the assembly:

Brothers and sisters (Brethren),
now is the acceptable time,
the day of divine favor
and human salvation,
when death is destroyed
and eternal life has its beginning;

it is the time in the vineyard of the Lord,
when, at the planting of the new vines,
the old vines are pruned,
that they may bear more fruit.

Each of us confesses that we are sinners,
and, when encouraged to repentance
by the example of others,
and moved by their prayers,
we testify and say:
"My transgressions, truly I know them;
my sin is always before me.
Turn away your face from my sins, O Lord,
and blot out all my guilt.
Restore in me the joy of your salvation;
sustain in me a willing spirit."

Therefore, as we humbly implore
divine mercy with a contrite heart,
may the mercy of the Lord come to our aid
so that we, who formerly displeased
the Lord with our wrongdoing,
may rejoice with the risen One,
the author of our life,
now that we are pleasing to the Lord
in the land of the living.

Then the Priest sprinkles those present with holy water, while all sing (say):

Sprinkle me with hyssop, O Lord,
and I shall be cleansed;
wash me and I shall be whiter than snow.

Then the Priest says the prayer:

O God, most gracious in creating
the human race
and most merciful in restoring it,
who by the Blood of your Only Begotten Son
redeemed us,
deprived of eternal bliss
by the envy of the devil,
give life through your Holy Spirit
to those whom you do not wish to die
and lift up those you have reproved,
for you do not abandon those who stray.
May the humble and trusting confession
of these your children
move you, O Lord.
Heal their wounds.
Stretch out your saving hand
to those who have fallen,
lest your Church be deprived
of a portion of her body,
lest your flock suffer loss,
lest the enemy exult at the harm
inflicted on your family,
lest the second death take those reborn
in the cleansing waters of salvation.
To you, Lord, we therefore pour out
our humble prayers,
the tears of our heart.
Spare those who confess their sins,
so that turned from the way of error
to the paths of justice

they may never again be harmed
by new wounds.
Rather, may what your grace bestowed
and your mercy restored
remain for them always intact.
Through our Lord Jesus Christ, your Son,
who lives and reigns with you
in the unity of the Holy Spirit,
God, for ever and ever.

℟. Amen.

The celebration then ends with an appropriate liturgical song and the dismissal of the people.

SECOND EXAMPLE

"Penance prepares for a fuller participation in the Paschal Mystery of Christ for the salvation of the world"

14. a) After an appropriate liturgical song and the greeting by the minister, the faithful are briefly led to an understanding that they are connected with each other in sin and in repentance, so that each one should feel himself (herself) called to conversion for the sanctification of the whole community.

15. b) Prayer

My brothers and sisters,
let us pray that by penance
we may be united with Christ,
who was crucified for our sins,
and so share with all people
in his Resurrection.

Let us kneel (or: Bow your heads before God).

All pray in silence for a while.

Let us stand (or: Raise your heads).

1

O Lord, our God and Father,
who have given us life
through the Passion of your Son,
grant that, joined through penance
to his Death,
we may also be sharers, with all people,
in his Resurrection.
Through Christ our Lord.

℟. Amen.

Or:

2

Grant, almighty and merciful Father,
that, moved and strengthened
by your Spirit,
we may always carry in our bodies
the Death of Jesus,
that his life may also be shown forth in us.
Through Christ our Lord.

℟. Amen.

16. c) Readings

—Like a meek lamb, the Servant of the Lord takes up and bears the sins of the people, that by his wounds they may be healed. Through penance the disciples of Christ can weep for and expiate in themselves the sins of the whole world.

FIRST READING Is 53:1-7, 10-12

A reading from the Book of the Prophet Isaiah

Who would believe what we have heard?
To whom has the arm of the LORD been revealed?
He grew up like a sapling before him,
like a shoot from the parched earth;
There was in him no stately bearing to make us look at him,
nor appearance that would attract us to him.
He was spurned and avoided by people,
a man of suffering, accustomed to infirmity,
One of those from whom people hide their faces,
spurned, and we held him in no esteem.

A2

Yet it was our infirmities that he bore,
our sufferings that he endured,
While we thought of him as stricken,
as one smitten by God and afflicted.
But he was pierced for our offenses,
crushed for our sins;
Upon him was the chastisement that makes us whole,
by his stripes we were healed.
We had all gone astray like sheep,
each following his own way;
But the LORD laid upon him
the guilt of us all.

Though he was harshly treated, he submitted
and opened not his mouth;
Like a lamb led to the slaughter
or a sheep before the shearers,
he was silent and opened not his mouth.

But the Lord was pleased
to crush him in infirmity.

If he gives his life as an offering for sin,
he shall see his descendants in a long life,
and the will of the Lord shall be accomplished through him.

Because of his affliction
he shall see the light in fullness of days;
Through his suffering, my servant shall justify many,
and their guilt he shall bear.
Therefore I will give him his portion among the great,
and he shall divide the spoils with the mighty,
Because he surrendered himself to death
and was counted among the wicked;
And he shall take away the sins of many,
and win pardon for their offenses.

The word of the Lord.

—The Lord hears the prayer of Christ who dies on the Cross for our sins. His Death becomes the life of the whole world. The penance through which we die to our sins is the renewal of life in the Church and in the world.

RESPONSORIAL PSALM

Ps 22 (21):2-3, 7-9, 18-19, 20-22, 23-24, 25, 26-27, 28

℟. (20) O Lord, my strength, make haste to help me!

My God, my God, why have you forsaken me?
Why are you far from saving me,
so far from my words of anguish?
O my God, I call by day and you do not answer;
I call by night and I find no reprieve.—℟.

But I am a worm and no man,
scorned by everyone, despised by the people.
All who see me deride me;
they curl their lips, they toss their heads:
"He trusted in the LORD, let him save him;
let him release him, for in him he delights."—℟.

I can count every one of my bones.
They stare at me and gloat.
They divide my clothing among them,
they cast lots for my robe.—℟.

But you, O LORD, do not stay afar off;
my strength, make haste to help me!
Rescue my soul from the sword,
my life from the grip of the dog.
Save my life from the jaws of the lion,
my poor soul from the horns of wild bulls.—℟.

I will tell of your name to my kin,
and praise you in the midst of the assembly.
"You who fear the LORD, give him praise;
all descendants of Jacob, give him glory;
revere him, all you descendants of Israel.—℟.

For he has never despised
nor scorned the poverty of the poor.
From him he has not hidden his face,
but he heard him whenever he cried."—℟.

You are my praise in the great assembly.
My vows I will pay before those who fear him.
The poor shall eat and shall have their fill.
They shall praise the LORD, those who seek him.
May your hearts live on forever and ever!—℟.

All the earth shall remember and return to the LORD,
all families of the nations worship before him.
—℟.

—If we patiently bear afflictions, either of nature or of others, by imitating Christ, we can extinguish the hatred of the world with our love and overcome evil with good, so that our participation in the Passion of Christ may benefit the life of the world.

SECOND READING 1 Pt 2:20b-25

A reading from the first Letter of Saint Peter

Beloved:
If you are patient when you suffer for doing what is good,
this is a grace before God.
For to this you have been called,
because Christ also suffered for you,
leaving you an example that you should follow in his footsteps.
He committed no sin, and no deceit was found in his mouth.

When he was insulted, he returned no insult;
when he suffered, he did not threaten;
instead, he handed himself over to the one who judges justly.
He himself bore our sins in his body upon the Cross,
so that, free from sin, we might live for righteousness.
By his wounds you have been healed.
For you had gone astray like sheep,
but you have now returned to the shepherd and guardian of your souls.

The word of the Lord.

VERSE BEFORE THE GOSPEL

Glory to you, O Lord, who were handed over for our sins

and rose again for our justification.
Glory to you, O Lord.

Or an appropriate liturgical song may be sung.

—Jesus exhorts his disciples, that following his example (drinking his cup) they may become servants of their brothers and sisters and lay down their lives for them.

GOSPEL

Mk 10:32-45

(LONG FORM)

✠ A reading from the holy Gospel according to Mark

The disciples were on the way, going up to Jerusalem,
and Jesus went ahead of them.
They were amazed, and those who followed were afraid.
Taking the Twelve aside again, he began to tell them
what was going to happen to him.
"Behold, we are going up to Jerusalem, and the Son of Man
will be handed over to the chief priests and the scribes,
and they will condemn him to death
and hand him over to the Gentiles who will mock him,
spit upon him, scourge him, and put him to death,
but after three days he will rise."

Then James and John, the sons of Zebedee,
came to Jesus and said to him,
"Teacher, we want you to do for us whatever we ask of you."

He replied, "What do you wish me to do for you?"
They answered him,
"Grant that in your glory
we may sit one at your right and the other at your left."
Jesus said to them, "You do not know what you are asking.
Can you drink the chalice that I drink
or be baptized with the baptism with which I am baptized?"
They said to him, "We can."
Jesus said to them, "The chalice that I drink, you will drink,
and with the baptism with which I am baptized, you will be baptized;
but to sit at my right or at my left is not mine to give
but is for those for whom it has been prepared."
When the ten heard this, they became indignant at James and John.
Jesus summoned them and said to them,
"You know that those who are recognized as rulers over the Gentiles
lord it over them,
and their great ones make their authority over them felt.
But it shall not be so among you.
Rather, whoever wishes to be great among you will be your servant;
whoever wishes to be first among you will be the slave of all.
For the Son of Man did not come to be served but to serve
and to give his life as a ransom for many."
The Gospel of the Lord.

Or:

Mk 10:32-34, 42-45

(SHORT FORM)

✠ A reading from the holy Gospel according to Mark

The disciples were on the way, going up to Jerusalem,
and Jesus went ahead of them.
They were amazed, and those who followed were afraid.
Taking the Twelve aside again, he began to tell them
what was going to happen to him.
"Behold, we are going up to Jerusalem, and the Son of Man
will be handed over to the chief priests and the scribes,
and they will condemn him to death
and hand him over to the Gentiles who will mock him,
spit upon him, scourge him, and put him to death,
but after three days he will rise."

Jesus summoned them and said to them,
"You know that those who are recognized as rulers over the Gentiles
lord it over them,
and their great ones make their authority over them felt.
But it shall not be so among you.
Rather, whoever wishes to be great among you will be your servant;
whoever wishes to be first among you will be the slave of all.
For the Son of Man did not come to be served but to serve
and to give his life as a ransom for many."

The Gospel of the Lord.

17. d) The Homily may address:

—sin, by which we offend God and also Christ's Body, that is the Church, whose members we became in Baptism;

—sin as a failure of love for Christ who in his Paschal Mystery loved us to the end;

—the effect we have on each other in doing good or choosing evil;

—the mystery of vicarious satisfaction, by which Christ himself bore our sins, so that by his wounds we would be healed (cf. Is 53; 1 Pt 2:24);

—the social and ecclesial aspect of penance, by which individuals share in the work of converting the whole community;

—the celebration of Easter as the feast of the Christian community, which is renewing itself by the conversion or repentance of each member, so that it may become a clearer sign of salvation in the world.

18. e) Examination of Conscience

After the Homily, the examination of conscience takes place; a sample text is found in Appendix III, p. 348. A period of silence should always be included, so that each person may examine his (her) conscience in a more personal manner.

19. f) Penitential Act

After the examination of conscience, all recite together:

I confess to almighty God
and to you, my brothers and sisters,

that I have greatly sinned,
in my thoughts and in my words,
in what I have done
and in what I have failed to do,

And, striking their breast, they say:

through my fault, through my fault,
through my most grievous fault;

Then they continue:

therefore I ask blessed Mary, ever-Virgin,
all the Angels and Saints,
and you, my brothers and sisters,
to pray for me to the Lord our God.

—Then as a sign of conversion and charity toward others, it should be suggested that the faithful give something to help the poor to celebrate the feast of Easter with joy; or they might visit the sick, or make up for some injustice in the community, or perform similar works.

—Finally, the Lord's Prayer may be sung or said, which the Priest concludes in this way:

**Deliver us, Father, from every evil,
and through the blessed Passion
of your Son,
to which we are joined through penance,
make us share joyfully in his Resurrection.
Through Christ our Lord.**

℟. Amen.

When the circumstances suggest, the general confession may be followed by some form of devotion such as Adoration of the Cross or the Stations of the Cross, according to local customs and the wishes of the people.

At the end, an appropriate liturgical song is sung, and the people are sent away with a blessing.

II. Penitential Celebration during Advent

20. a) After a liturgical song and the greeting, the meaning of the celebration is explained briefly in these or similar words:

1

Brothers and sisters (Brethren),
the season of Advent prepares us
to celebrate
the mystery of the Lord's Incarnation,
in which our salvation has its beginning;
at the same time,
it stirs us to look forward to
the Second Coming of the Lord,
by which the history of our salvation
will be completed.
Moreover, when the Lord comes
to each of us at the hour of death,
he should find us watching,
as it says in the Gospel:
"Blessed are those servants
whom the Lord finds awake
at his coming" (Luke 12:37).

May this penitential celebration purify us
and make us better prepared
for this coming of the Lord,
which we shall celebrate
in the sacred mysteries.

Or:

2 (Romans 13:11-12)

Brothers and sisters (Brethren),
now is the hour to rise from sleep.
For salvation is nearer to us now
than when we first believed.
The night has gone,
and the day is drawing near;
let us therefore cast off
the works of darkness
and put on the armor of light.

21. b) Prayer

Let us pray, brothers and sisters,
that the Advent of the Lord,
whose mystery we shall celebrate
in the coming solemnities,
will find us watching and prepared.

All pray in silence for a while.

1

We ask pardon for our offenses,
O God, Creator of the heavens,
so that, as we await the appearing
of our Redeemer,

we may be found worthy
to receive forgiveness for our sins.
Through Christ our Lord.

℟. Amen.

Or:

2

Exalted Son of God,
Creator and sinless Savior
of the human race,
come now, we pray,
from the Virgin undefiled,
come forth to redeem the world,
that we may experience
deliverance from our sins
by that grace through which
you were pleased
to become one like us except for sin.
Who live and reign for ever and ever.

℟. Amen.

22. c) Readings

—The coming of the Lord brings with it judgment. We ourselves choose now punishment or reward through our deeds. When the Lord appears, then our choice will be manifest. Repentance is the moment of choice and decision.

FIRST READING Mal 3:1-7a

A reading from the
Book of the Prophet Malachi

Lo, I am sending my messenger
to prepare the way before me;
And suddenly there will come to the temple
the LORD whom you seek,
And the messenger of the covenant whom you desire.
Yes, he is coming, says the LORD of hosts.
But who will endure the day of his coming?
And who can stand when he appears?
For he is like the refiner's fire,
or like the fuller's lye.
He will sit refining and purifying silver,
and he will purify the sons of Levi,
Refining them like gold or like silver
that they may offer due sacrifice to the LORD.
Then the sacrifice of Judah and Jerusalem
will please the LORD,
as in days of old, as in years gone by.
I will draw near to you for judgment,
and I will be swift to bear witness
Against the sorcerers, adulterers, and perjurers,
those who defraud the hired man of his wages,
Against those who defraud widows and orphans;
those who turn aside the stranger,
and those who do not fear me, says the LORD of hosts.

Surely I, the LORD, do not change,
nor do you cease to be sons of Jacob.
Since the days of your fathers you have turned aside
from my statutes, and have not kept them.
Return to me, and I will return to you,
says the LORD of hosts.

The word of the Lord.

—God sent his Son into the world not to condemn the world but to save it. Therefore the advent of the Lord, which we now celebrate in mystery, is the advent of salvation. This penitential service takes place in the hope of that salvation, so that rejoicing we may celebrate the Nativity of the Lord and hasten to meet him.

RESPONSORIAL PSALM

Ps 85 (84):2-4, 5-6, 7-8, 9-10, 11-12, 13-14

℟. (8) Show us, O Lord, your mercy, and grant us your salvation.

O LORD, you have favored your land,
and brought back the captives of Jacob.
You forgave the guilt of your people,
and covered all their sins.
You averted all your rage;
you turned back the heat of your anger.—℟.

Bring us back, O God, our savior!
Put an end to your grievance against us.
Will you be angry with us forever?
Will your anger last from age to age?—℟.

Will you not restore again our life,
that your people may rejoice in you?
Show us, O LORD, your mercy,
and grant us your salvation.—℟.

I will hear what the LORD God speaks;
he speaks of peace for his people and his faithful,
and those who turn their hearts to him.
His salvation is near for those who fear him,
and his glory will dwell in our land.—℟.

Mercy and faithfulness have met;
justice and peace have kissed.
Faithfulness shall spring from the earth,
and justice look down from heaven.—℟.

Also the LORD will bestow his bounty,
and our earth shall yield its increase.
Righteousness will march before him,
and guide his steps on the way.—℟.

—Through his advent the Lord Jesus will lead us into a new life and into a new world. Even now the Church is a living sign of this holy city which will be revealed in the future: but we exclude ourselves from it through sin.

SECOND READING Rev 21:1-12

A reading from the Book of Revelation

I, John, saw a new heaven and a new earth.
The former heaven and the former earth had passed away,
and the sea was no more.
I also saw the holy city, a new Jerusalem,
coming down out of heaven from God,
prepared as a bride adorned for her husband.
I heard a loud voice from the throne saying,
"Behold, God's dwelling is with the human race.
He will dwell with them and they will be his people
and God himself will always be with them as their God.
He will wipe every tear from their eyes,
and there shall be no more death or mourning, wailing or pain,
for the old order has passed away."

The one who sat on the throne said,
"Behold, I make all things new."
Then he said, "Write these words down,
for they are trustworthy and true."

He said to me,"They are accomplished.
I am the Alpha and the Omega,
the beginning and the end.
To the thirsty I will give a gift
from the spring of life-giving water.
The victor will inherit these gifts,
and I shall be his God,
and he will be my son.
But as for cowards, the unfaithful, the depraved,
murderers, the unchaste, sorcerers, idol-worshipers,
and deceivers of every sort,
their lot is in the burning pool of fire and sulfur,
which is the second death."

One of the seven angels who held the seven bowls
filled with the seven last plagues
came and said to me,
"Come here. I will show you the bride, the wife of the Lamb."
He took me in spirit to a great, high mountain
and showed me the holy city Jerusalem
coming down out of heaven from God.
It gleamed with the splendor of God.
Its radiance was like that of a precious stone,
like jasper, clear as crystal.
It had a massive, high wall, with twelve gates
where twelve angels were stationed
and on which names were inscribed,
the names of the twelve tribes of the children of Israel.

The word of the Lord.

VERSE BEFORE THE GOSPEL

1 Rev 22:12, 20

The Lord says: "Behold I am coming quickly,
and my reward is with me."
Come, Lord Jesus.

Or:

2 Rev 22:17, 20

The Spirit and the Bride say: "Come."
And whoever hears says: "Come."
Come, Lord Jesus.

Or another appropriate liturgical song may be sung.

A2

—As in the days of John the Baptist, so also today for us, the coming of the Lord is a time for conversion and penance, so that, when he comes, we may receive salvation.

GOSPEL

1 Mt 3:1-12

✠ A reading from the holy Gospel
according to Matthew

John the Baptist appeared, preaching in the desert
of Judea
and saying, "Repent, for the Kingdom of heaven
is at hand!"
It was of him that the prophet Isaiah had spoken
when he said:

A voice of one crying out in the desert,
"Prepare the way of the Lord,
make straight his paths."
John wore clothing made of camel's hair
and had a leather belt around his waist.
His food was locusts and wild honey.
At that time Jerusalem, all Judea,
and the whole region around the Jordan
were going out to him
and were being baptized by him in the Jordan River
as they acknowledged their sins.

When he saw many of the Pharisees and Sadducees coming to his baptism, he said to them, "You brood of vipers!
Who warned you to flee from the coming wrath?
Produce good fruit as evidence of your repentance.
And do not presume to say to yourselves,
'We have Abraham as our father.'
For I tell you,
God can raise up children to Abraham from these stones.
Even now the ax lies at the root of the trees.
Therefore every tree that does not bear good fruit
will be cut down and thrown into the fire.
I am baptizing you with water, for repentance,
but the one who is coming after me is mightier than I.
I am not worthy to carry his sandals.
He will baptize you with the Holy Spirit and fire.
His winnowing fan is in his hand.
He will clear his threshing floor
and gather his wheat into his barn,
but the chaff he will burn with unquenchable fire."

The Gospel of the Lord.

2 Lk 3:3-17

✠ A reading from the holy Gospel
according to Luke

In the fifteenth year of the reign of Tiberius Caesar,
when Pontius Pilate was governor of Judea,
and Herod was tetrarch of Galilee,
and his brother Philip tetrarch of the region of Ituraea and Trachonitis,
and Lysanias was tetrarch of Abilene,
during the high priesthood of Annas and Caiaphas,
the word of God came to John the son of Zechariah in the desert.
John went throughout the whole region of the Jordan,
proclaiming a baptism of repentance for the forgiveness of sins,
as it is written in the book of the words of the prophet Isaiah:
A voice of one crying out in the desert:
"Prepare the way of the Lord,
make straight his paths.
Every valley shall be filled
and every mountain and hill shall be made low.
The winding roads shall be made straight,
and the rough ways made smooth,
and all flesh shall see the salvation of God."
The crowds asked John the Baptist,
"What should we do?"
He said to them in reply,
"Whoever has two cloaks
should share with the person who has none.
And whoever has food should do likewise."
Even tax collectors came to be baptized and they said to him,
"Teacher, what should we do?"

He answered them,
"Stop collecting more than what is prescribed."
Soldiers also asked him,
"And what is it that we should do?"
He told them,
"Do not practice extortion,
do not falsely accuse anyone,
and be satisfied with your wages."

Now the people were filled with expectation,
and all were asking in their hearts
whether John might be the Christ.
John answered them all, saying,
"I am baptizing you with water,
but one mightier than I is coming.
I am not worthy to loosen the thongs of his sandals.
He will baptize you with the Holy Spirit and fire.
His winnowing fan is in his hand to clear his threshing floor
and to gather the wheat into his barn,
but the chaff he will burn with unquenchable fire."

The Gospel of the Lord.

---

23. d) After the Homily, the examination of conscience then takes place; a sample text is found in Appendix III, p. 348. A period of silence should always be included, so that each person may examine his (her) conscience in a more personal manner.

24. e) Penitential Act

After the examination of conscience, the Penitential Act takes place, for example, by saying the I confess to almighty God or using the intercessions as in Appendix II, no. 60. Afterwards, the Lord's Prayer is said or sung and is concluded by the presiding minister in this way:

1

O God, who, in creating light
at the beginning of the world,
scattered the thick clouds of darkness,
we pray that Christ,
the very Author of light,
whose coming you prepared
before the ages,
will now come forth,
so that a people freed from the ancient error
and made ready by good works
may go out to meet your Son.
Who lives and reigns for ever and ever.

℟. Amen.

Or:

2

Almighty and eternal God,
who by the Incarnation
of your Only Begotten Son
mercifully reconciled the world
to your majesty,
grant, we pray,
that the clouds of sin may flee
from hearts made tranquil
and that, as the light grows stronger,
the mysteries of the Lord's Nativity
may always be celebrated
with unsullied joy.
Through Christ our Lord.

℟. Amen.

At the end, an appropriate liturgical song is sung, and the people are sent away with a greeting or blessing.

III. Common Penitential Celebrations

I. Sin and Conversion

25. a) After an appropriate liturgical song (e.g., Psalm 139 [138]: 1-12, 16, 23-24, no. 146) and greeting, the minister who presides at the celebration briefly explains the meaning of the readings. Then he invites all to pray. After a period of silence, he concludes the prayer in this way:

Lord Jesus,
when Peter denied you three times
you turned and looked at him,
that he might weep for his sin
and return to you with all his heart.
Look upon us and move our hearts,
that we may return to you
and follow you faithfully all our lives.
Who live and reign for ever and ever.

℟. Amen.

26. b) Readings

FIRST READING — Lk 22:31-34

"I tell you, Peter, before the cock crows this day, you will deny three times that you know me."

✠ **A reading from the holy Gospel according to Luke**

Jesus said,
"Simon, Simon, behold Satan has demanded
to sift all of you like wheat,
but I have prayed that your own faith may not fail;
and once you have turned back,
you must strengthen your brothers."
He said to him,
"Lord, I am prepared to go to prison and to die with you."
But he replied,
"I tell you, Peter, before the cock crows this day,
you will deny three times that you know me."

The Gospel of the Lord.

A short period of silence follows the reading.

SECOND READING Lk 22:54-62

Peter went out and began to weep bitterly.

✠ A reading from the holy Gospel according to Luke

After arresting Jesus they led him away
and took him into the house of the high priest;
Peter was following at a distance.
They lit a fire in the middle of the courtyard and sat around it,
and Peter sat down with them.
When a maid saw him seated in the light,
she looked intently at him and said,
"This man too was with him."
But he denied it saying,
"Woman, I do not know him."
A short while later someone else saw him and said,
"You too are one of them";
but Peter answered,"My friend, I am not."

About an hour later, still another insisted,
"Assuredly, this man too was with him,
for he also is a Galilean."
But Peter said,
"My friend, I do not know what you are talking about."
Just as he was saying this, the cock crowed,
and the Lord turned and looked at Peter;
and Peter remembered the word of the Lord,
how he had said to him,
"Before the cock crows today, you will deny me three times."
He went out and began to weep bitterly.

The Gospel of the Lord.

RESPONSORIAL PSALM

Ps 31 (30):10, 15-17, 20

℟. (17b) Save me, Lord, in your merciful love.

Have mercy on me, O LORD,
for I am in distress.
My eyes are wasted with grief,
my soul and my body.—℟.

As for me, I trust in you, O LORD;
I say, "You are my God.
There in your hands is my lot,
from the hands of my enemies deliver me,
and from those who pursue me.
Let your face shine on your servant.
Save me in your merciful love.—℟.

How great is the goodness, LORD,
that you keep for those who fear you,
that you show to those who trust you
in the sight of the children of Adam.—℟.

Or Ps 51 (50) (no. 139) or another liturgical song.

GOSPEL

Jn 21:15-19

"Simon, son of John, do you love me?"

✠ **A reading from the holy Gospel according to John**

After Jesus had revealed himself to his disciples and eaten breakfast with them,
he said to Simon Peter,
"Simon, son of John, do you love me more than these?"
Simon Peter answered him, "Yes, Lord, you know that I love you."
Jesus said to him, "Feed my lambs."
He then said to Simon Peter a second time,
"Simon, son of John, do you love me?"
Simon Peter answered him, "Yes, Lord, you know that I love you."
He said to him, "Tend my sheep."
He said to him the third time,
"Simon, son of John, do you love me?"
Peter was distressed that he had said to him a third time,
"Do you love me?" and he said to him,
"Lord, you know everything; you know that I love you."
Jesus said to him, "Feed my sheep.
Amen, amen, I say to you, when you were younger,
you used to dress yourself and go where you wanted;
but when you grow old, you will stretch out your hands,
and someone else will dress you
and lead you where you do not want to go."

He said this signifying by what kind of death he would glorify God.
And when he had said this, he said to him, "Follow me."
The Gospel of the Lord.

---

27. c) The Homily may address:

—the trust we must put in God's grace, not in our own powers;

—the faithfulness, by which we the baptized must live as true disciples of the Lord;

—our weakness, by which we often fall into sin and refuse to give witness to the Gospel;

—the mercy of the Lord, who welcomes us back as friends after we have sinned, if we turn to him with our whole heart.

28. d) Examination of Conscience

After the Homily, the examination of conscience takes place; a sample text is found in Appendix III, p. 348. A period of silence should always be included, so that each person may examine his (her) conscience in a more personal manner.

29. e) Penitential Act

After the examination of conscience, the presiding minister invites all to prayer in these or similar words:

God proves his love for us,
in that while we were still sinners,
he first loved us and took pity on us.

Let us therefore turn to him
with all our heart
and, with Peter, humbly confess our love,
as we say:

℟. Lord, you know all things; you know that I love you.

It is desirable for a short period of silence to come between one invocation and the next one. It is appropriate that each invocation be said by a different member of the faithful, the rest answering.

—Like Peter, Lord,
we too have trusted in ourselves
rather than in your grace;
but turn to us, Lord, and have mercy on us.

℟. Lord, you know all things; you know that I love you.

—We have acted neither with humility
nor with prudence
and so have fallen into temptation;
but turn to us, Lord, and have mercy on us.

℟. Lord, you know all things; you know that I love you.

—We were proud and considered ourselves
better than others;
but turn to us, Lord, and have mercy on us.

℟. Lord, you know all things; you know that I love you.

—We have at times been pleased
rather than saddened
by the fall of our brothers and sisters;
but turn to us, Lord, and have mercy on us.

℟. Lord, you know all things; you know that I love you.

—We have often shown contempt,
rather than offered help
to those in difficulty;
but turn to us, Lord, and have mercy on us.

℟. Lord, you know all things; you know that I love you.

—At times, through fear,
we have refused to bear witness
to truth and justice;
but turn to us, Lord, and have mercy on us.

℟. Lord, you know all things; you know that I love you.

—We have often been unfaithful
to our baptismal promises,
by which we were made your disciples;
but turn to us, Lord, and have mercy on us.

℟. Lord, you know all things; you know that I love you.

Let us now address our prayer to the Father,
and, as Christ taught us,
ask him to forgive our sins:

**Our Father, who art in heaven,
hallowed be thy name;
thy kingdom come,
thy will be done
on earth as it is in heaven.
Give us this day our daily bread,
and forgive us our trespasses,
as we forgive those who trespass against us;
and lead us not into temptation,
but deliver us from evil.**

30. f) Then, after an appropriate liturgical song, the minister who presides at the celebration says the concluding prayer and dismisses the people:

**Lord Jesus, our Savior,
who called Peter to be an Apostle
and, after his failure and repentance,
confirmed him again as your friend
and the Prince of the Apostles,
turn to us and look upon us with favor,
that, following the example of Peter,
we may turn again to you after our sins
and follow you henceforth
with greater love.
Who live and reign for ever and ever.**

℟. Amen.

II. The Son Returns to the Father

31. a) After an appropriate liturgical song and a greeting, the minister explains the theme of the celebration to those present. Then the minister invites all to pray, and, after a period of silence, concludes by saying:

Lord God almighty,
you are the Father of all.
You made man and woman,
that they should always be with you
in your house,
for the praise of your glory.

Open our hearts to hear your voice,
that we, who have turned away from you
by sinning,
may now return to you with all our heart.
May we acknowledge you to be our Father,
full of mercy to all who call on you,
rebuking us that we may turn from evil,
and forgiving us all our sins.
Give us again the joy of your salvation,
that, turning back to you,
we may rejoice in the banquet
of your house,
now and always and for ever and ever.

℟. Amen.

32. b) Readings

FIRST READING Eph 1:3-7

He destined us for adoption to himself.

A reading from the Letter of
Saint Paul to the Ephesians

Blessed be the God and Father of our Lord Jesus
Christ,
who has blessed us in Christ
with every spiritual blessing in the heavens,

as he chose us in him, before the foundation of the world,
to be holy and without blemish before him.
In love he destined us for adoption to himself through Jesus Christ,
in accord with the favor of his will,
for the praise of the glory of his grace
that he granted us in the beloved.

The word of the Lord.

RESPONSORIAL PSALM

Ps 27 (26):1, 4, 7-8b, 8c-9c, 9d-10, 13-14

℟. (1a) The Lord is my light and my salvation.

The LORD is my light and my salvation;
whom shall I fear?
The LORD is the stronghold of my life;
whom should I dread?—℟.

There is one thing I ask of the LORD,
only this do I seek:
to live in the house of the LORD
all the days of my life,
to gaze on the beauty of the LORD,
to inquire at his temple.—℟.

O LORD, hear my voice when I call;
have mercy and answer me.
Of you my heart has spoken,
"Seek his face."—℟.

It is your face, O LORD, that I seek;
hide not your face from me.
Dismiss not your servant in anger;
you have been my help.—℟.

Do not abandon or forsake me,
O God, my Savior!

Though father and mother forsake me,
the LORD will receive me.—℟.

I believe I shall see the LORD's goodness
in the land of the living.
Wait for the LORD; be strong;
be stouthearted, and wait for the LORD!—℟.

GOSPEL Lk 15:11-32

*His father caught sight of him,
and was filled with compassion.*

✠ A reading from the holy Gospel
according to Luke

Jesus addressed this parable to them:
"A man had two sons, and the younger son said to his father,
'Father, give me the share of your estate that should come to me.'
So the father divided the property between them.
After a few days, the younger son collected all his belongings
and set off to a distant country
where he squandered his inheritance on a life of dissipation.
When he had freely spent everything,
a severe famine struck that country,
and he found himself in dire need.
So he hired himself out to one of the local citizens
who sent him to his farm to tend the swine.
And he longed to eat his fill of the pods on which the swine fed,
but nobody gave him any.
Coming to his senses he thought,
'How many of my father's hired workers

have more than enough food to eat,
but here am I, dying from hunger.
I shall get up and go to my father and I shall say to him,
"Father, I have sinned against heaven and against you.
I no longer deserve to be called your son;
treat me as you would treat one of your hired workers." '
So he got up and went back to his father.
While he was still a long way off,
his father caught sight of him, and was filled with compassion.
He ran to his son, embraced him and kissed him.
His son said to him,
'Father, I have sinned against heaven and against you;
I no longer deserve to be called your son.'
But his father ordered his servants,
'Quickly, bring the finest robe and put it on him;
put a ring on his finger and sandals on his feet.
Take the fattened calf and slaughter it.
Then let us celebrate with a feast,
because this son of mine was dead, and has come to life again;
he was lost, and has been found.'
Then the celebration began.
Now the older son had been out in the field
and, on his way back, as he neared the house,
he heard the sound of music and dancing.
He called one of the servants and asked what this might mean.
The servant said to him,
'Your brother has returned
and your father has slaughtered the fattened calf
because he has him back safe and sound.'

He became angry,
and when he refused to enter the house,
his father came out and pleaded with him.
He said to his father in reply,
'Look, all these years I served you
and not once did I disobey your orders;
yet you never gave me even a young goat to feast on with my friends.
But when your son returns
who swallowed up your property with prostitutes,
for him you slaughter the fattened calf.'
He said to him,
'My son, you are here with me always;
everything I have is yours.
But now we must celebrate and rejoice,
because your brother was dead and has come to life again;
he was lost and has been found.' "

The Gospel of the Lord.

---

33. c) The Homily may address:

—sin as a turning away from the filial love toward God our Father;

—the infinite mercy of our Father for his children who have sinned;

—the nature of true conversion;

—the forgiveness we should always extend to our brothers and sisters;

—the Eucharistic Banquet as the culmination of our reconciliation with the Church and with God.

34. d) Examination of Conscience

After the Homily, the examination of conscience takes place; a sample text is found in Appendix III, p. 348. A period of silence should always be included, so that each person may examine his (her) conscience in a more personal manner.

35. e) Penitential Act

After the examination of conscience, the presiding minister invites all to pray:

Our God is a merciful God,
slow to anger and rich in patience,
who welcomes us back
as the father welcomes his son from afar.
Let us pray to him with confidence,
as we say:

℟. We are not worthy to be called your children.

—Because we are sinners before you
and have misused your gifts:

℟. We are not worthy to be called your children.

—Because we are sinners before you
and have wandered far from you
in mind and heart:

℟. We are not worthy to be called your children.

—Because we are sinners before you
and have been unmindful of your love:

℟. We are not worthy to be called your children.

—Because we are sinners before you
and have sought our pleasure,
rather than our good
and that of our brothers and sisters:

℟. We are not worthy to be called your children.

—Because we are sinners before you
and have taken little care
of our brothers and sisters:

℟. We are not worthy to be called your children.

—Because we are sinners before you
and were slow to forgive
our brothers and sisters:

℟. We are not worthy to be called your children.

—Because we are sinners before you
and have been unmindful of your mercy,
by which you received us back
time and time again:

℟. We are not worthy to be called your children.

Other invocations may be added by those present. It is preferable for a short period of silence to come between one invocation and the next one. It is also appropriate that each invocation be said by a different member of the faithful.

Let us now call upon our Father
in the words that Jesus taught us,
and ask him to forgive us our sins:

Our Father, who art in heaven,
hallowed be thy name;
thy kingdom come,
thy will be done
on earth as it is in heaven.
Give us this day our daily bread,
and forgive us our trespasses,
as we forgive those who trespass against us;
and lead us not into temptation,
but deliver us from evil.

36. f) Then, after an appropriate liturgical song, the minister who presides at the celebration says the concluding prayer and dismisses the people:

O God our Father,
who predestined us
to be your adopted children,
that we might be holy in your sight
and rejoice for ever in your house,
accept us and keep us in your love,
that we may live with joy and charity
in your holy Church.
Through Christ our Lord.

℟. Amen.

III. The Beatitudes

37. a) After an appropriate liturgical song and greeting, the minister who presides at the celebration explains to those present the meaning of the readings and invites them to pray. After a period of silence, he concludes the prayer:

Open our hearts, O Lord,
to hear your voice today,
that, welcoming the Gospel of your Son,
we may,
through his Death and Resurrection,
come to walk in newness of life.
Through Christ our Lord.

℟. Amen.

38. b) Readings

FIRST READING 1 Jn 1:5-9

If we say, "We are without sin,"
we deceive ourselves.

A reading from the first Letter of Saint John

Beloved:
This is the message that we have heard from Jesus Christ
and proclaim to you: God is light,
and in him there is no darkness at all.
If we say, "We have fellowship with him,"
while we continue to walk in darkness,
we lie and do not act in truth.
But if we walk in the light as he is in the light,
then we have fellowship with one another,

and the Blood of his Son Jesus cleanses us from all sin.
If we say, "We are without sin," we deceive ourselves,
and the truth is not in us.
If we acknowledge our sins, he is faithful and just
and will forgive our sins and cleanse us from every wrongdoing.

The word of the Lord.

RESPONSORIAL PSALM

Ps 146 (145):5-7a, 7b-8b, 8c-10

℟. (cf. 5) Blessed are they who hope in the Lord.

Blessed is he who is helped by Jacob's God,
whose hope is in the LORD his God,
who made the heavens and the earth,
the seas and all they contain,
who preserves fidelity forever,
who does justice to those who are oppressed.—℟.

It is he who gives bread to the hungry,
the LORD who sets prisoners free,
the LORD who opens the eyes of the blind,
the LORD who raises up those who are bowed down.—℟.

It is the LORD who loves the just,
the LORD who protects the stranger
and upholds the orphan and the widow,
but thwarts the path of the wicked.
The LORD will reign forever,
your God, O Zion, from age to age.—℟.

GOSPEL

Mt 5:1-10

Blessed are the poor in spirit,
for theirs is the Kingdom of heaven.

✠ **A reading from the holy Gospel according to Matthew**

When Jesus saw the crowds, he went up the mountain, and after he had sat down, his disciples came to him.
He began to teach them, saying:

"Blessed are the poor in spirit,
for theirs is the Kingdom of heaven.
Blessed are they who mourn,
for they will be comforted.
Blessed are the meek,
for they will inherit the land.
Blessed are they who hunger and thirst for righteousness,
for they will be satisfied.
Blessed are the merciful,
for they will be shown mercy.
Blessed are the clean of heart,
for they will see God.
Blessed are the peacemakers,
for they will be called children of God.
Blessed are they who are persecuted for the sake of righteousness,
for theirs is the Kingdom of heaven."

The Gospel of the Lord.

---

39. c) The Homily may address:

—sin, by which we, forgetting the commandments of Christ, act contrary to the teaching of the Beatitudes of the Gospel;

—the firmness of our faith in the words of Jesus;

—our faithfulness in imitating Christ not only in our private lives, as well as in the Christian community, but also in human society;

—each Beatitude.

40. d) Examination of Conscience

After the Homily, the examination of conscience takes place; a sample text is found in Appendix III, p. 348. A period of silence should always be included, so that each person may examine his (her) conscience in a more personal manner.

41. e) Penitential Act

After the examination of conscience, the presiding minister invites all to prayer in these or similar words:

**Brothers and sisters:
Jesus Christ left us an example,
that we should follow in his footsteps.**

**Let us direct our prayer to him
in all humility and trust,
that he will purify our hearts
and grant us to live in accordance
with his Gospel:**

**—Lord Jesus Christ, you said:
"Blessed are the poor in spirit,
for theirs is the Kingdom of Heaven";
but we are overly concerned with riches
and even seek them unjustly.
Lamb of God, you take away
the sin of the world,**

℟. have mercy on us.

—Lord Jesus Christ, you said:
"Blessed are the meek,
for they shall possess the earth";
but we are violent towards one another
and our world is full of discord and wars.
Lamb of God, you take away
the sin of the world,

℟. have mercy on us.

—Lord Jesus Christ, you said:
"Blessed are those who mourn,
for they shall be comforted";
but we are impatient
with our own afflictions
and care little about
our afflicted brothers and sisters.
Lamb of God, you take away
the sin of the world,

℟. have mercy on us.

—Lord Jesus Christ, you said:
"Blessed are those
who hunger and thirst for justice,
for they shall be satisfied";
but we thirst little for you,
the fount of all holiness
and are indifferent to justice
in private and public life.
Lamb of God, you take away
the sin of the world,

℟. have mercy on us.

—Lord Jesus Christ, you said:
"Blessed are the merciful,
for they shall receive mercy";
but we are unwilling
to forgive our brothers and sisters
and are severe in judging our neighbors.
Lamb of God, you take away
the sin of the world,

℟. have mercy on us.

—Lord Jesus Christ, you said:
"Blessed are the pure in heart,
for they shall see God";
but we are slaves
to our wayward desires and sensuality,
not daring to raise our eyes to you.
Lamb of God, you take away
the sin of the world,

℟. have mercy on us.

—Lord Jesus Christ, you said:
"Blessed are the peacemakers,
for they shall be called children of God";
but we are unable to make peace
in our families,
in society, and in the world.
Lamb of God, you take away
the sin of the world,

℟. have mercy on us.

—Lord Jesus Christ, you said:
"Blessed are those who suffer persecution
for justice's sake,

for theirs is the Kingdom of Heaven";
but instead of suffering willingly
for justice's sake,
we prefer to act unjustly
and we discriminate
against our brothers and sisters,
oppressing and persecuting them.
Lamb of God, you take away
the sin of the world,

℟. have mercy on us.

Now let us call upon the Lord our Father,
that he will deliver us from evil
and make us worthy of his Kingdom:

Our Father, who art in heaven,
hallowed be thy name;
thy kingdom come,
thy will be done
on earth as it is in heaven.
Give us this day our daily bread,
and forgive us our trespasses,
as we forgive those who trespass against us;
and lead us not into temptation,
but deliver us from evil.

42. f) After an appropriate liturgical song, the minister who presides at the celebration says the concluding prayer and dismisses the people:

Lord Jesus Christ,
meek and humble of heart,
maker of peace and merciful,
poor and slain for righteousness' sake,

who came into glory through the Cross
to show us the way of salvation,
grant that
we may joyfully accept your Gospel
and live according to your example
as coheirs and sharers in your Kingdom.
Who live and reign for ever and ever.

℟. Amen.

IV. For Children

43. This example of a penitential celebration is suitable for younger children, including those who have not yet participated in a sacramental confession.

THEME

"God comes to look for us"

44. The penitential celebration should be prepared with the children themselves, so that they will thereby already understand the meaning and purpose of such a celebration, be familiar with the songs, have at least an elementary knowledge of the text of Sacred Scripture to be read, and know the text they are to say themselves and in what order.

45. a) Greeting

When the children are gathered in the church or some other suitable place, the celebrant greets them in a friendly manner. Briefly he reminds them about the purpose of the celebration and aspects which pertain to the order of the celebration. After the greeting, an introductory liturgical song may be sung.

46. b) Reading

The celebrant may give a short introduction in these or similar words:

My dear children,
we have all been made
sons and daughters of God by Baptism.
God loves us as a Father
and teaches us to love him
with our whole heart.
And he also wants us to be good
to one another,
so that we may all live happily together.

Yet, people do not always act
according to God's will.
They say: "I won't obey!
I'll do what I want!"
They do not obey God and are not willing
to listen to his voice.
And we often do the same.

This is what we call sin,
when we turn away from God,
and, if our sin is truly serious,
we separate ourselves from God completely.

How does God act,
when people turn away from him?
What does he do when we leave
the right path and risk losing our life?
When he is offended
he does not turn away from us, does he?

Let us listen to what the Lord says to us:

47. Only one text of Sacred Scripture should be read.

GOSPEL

Lk 15:1-7

✠ **A reading from the holy Gospel according to Luke**

Tax collectors and sinners were all drawing near to listen to Jesus,
but the Pharisees and scribes began to complain, saying,
"This man welcomes sinners and eats with them."
So to them Jesus addressed this parable.
"What man among you having a hundred sheep and losing one of them
would not leave the ninety-nine in the desert
and go after the lost one until he finds it?
And when he does find it,
he sets it on his shoulders with great joy
and, upon his arrival home,
he calls together his friends and neighbors and says to them,
'Rejoice with me because I have found my lost sheep.'
I tell you, in just the same way
there will be more joy in heaven over one sinner who repents
than over ninety-nine righteous people
who have no need of repentance."

The Gospel of the Lord.

---

48. c) Homily

The Homily should be short, particularly proclaiming God's love for us and preparing the ground for the examination of conscience.

49. d) Examination of Conscience

The examination should be adapted to the children's level of understanding by brief comments by the celebrant. A suitable period of silence should be included (cf. Appendix III, p. 348).

50. e) Penitential Act

The following litany may be said by the celebrant or by one or more of the children, alternating with all present. Before the responses, which may be sung, all should observe a brief pause.

O God our Father,
—We have often not acted
as your children should.

℟. Still you love us and look for us.

—We have behaved badly
to our parents and teachers.

℟. Still you love us and look for us.

—We have been mean
and spoken rudely to one another.

℟. Still you love us and look for us.

—We have been lazy at home
(and in school)
and not ready to help our parents
(brothers and sisters, other children).

℟. Still you love us and look for us.

—We have been selfish and told lies.

℟. Still you love us and look for us.

—We have not done good
when we had the chance.

℟. Still you love us and look for us.

And now, together with Jesus, our brother,
we turn to the Father
and ask him to forgive us our sins:

Our Father, who art in heaven,
hallowed be thy name;
thy kingdom come,
thy will be done
on earth as it is in heaven.
Give us this day our daily bread,
and forgive us our trespasses,
as we forgive those who trespass against us;
and lead us not into temptation,
but deliver us from evil.

51. f) Act of Contrition and Purpose of Amendment

Sorrow may be shown by some sign, for example, if it seems appropriate, individual children come to the altar or another suitable place with a candle and light it there; if necessary, a minister may help. Each child says:

Father, I am sorry
for all the bad I have done,
and the good I have failed to do.
I will sincerely try to do better,
especially . . . (here mention a particular resolution)
and to walk in your light.

In place of the candle, or in addition to it, the children may place the text of a prayer or resolution written on a piece of paper on the altar or on a table designated for this purpose.

If, however, the number of children or other circumstances do not allow for this, the celebrant asks the children present to say the above prayer together, along with a general resolution.

52. g) Prayer of the Celebrant

God our Father always searches for us
when we wander from the right path,
and he is ready to forgive
the wrong we have done.
And so, may almighty God
have mercy on us,
forgive us our sins,
and bring us to everlasting life.

℟. Amen.

53. The minister invites the children to express their thanks to God. They may do this by an appropriate liturgical song.

Then the minister dismisses them.

V. For Young People

54. A penitential celebration with young people should be prepared, so that they themselves, insofar as it is possible, may, along with the celebrant, choose or compose the texts and liturgical songs. The readers, cantors, or choir should be chosen from among them.

THEME

"Renewal of our lives according to the Christian vocation"

55. a) The greeting may be given in these or similar words:

Dear brothers and sisters,
we have gathered to do penance
    and to renew our life.
This is not, as many people think,
    something only difficult and sad,
but even an occasion for joy,
looking more to the future than to the past.
Through repentance
    God opens up for us a new way,
leading us more and more into
    the full freedom of the children of God.
Christ, calling us to conversion,
offers us a way
    into the Kingdom of his Father,
as he taught in the parable of the merchant,
who, when he had found
    the pearl of great price,
sold everything in order to buy it.
Guided by such good counsel,
we leave behind our former life,
that we may pursue a new life
    far more worthwhile.

Then a liturgical song is sung, which pertains to the call to a new life or to following God's call with an eager heart (e.g., Psalm 40 [39]:1-9).

Psalm 40 (39):2, 3, 4, 5, 6, 7, 8-9

℟. (8a, 9a) Behold, I have come to do your will.

I waited, I waited for the LORD,
and he stooped down to me;
he heard my cry.—℟.

He drew me from the deadly pit,
from the miry clay.
He set my feet upon a rock,
made my footsteps firm.—℟.

He put a new song into my mouth,
praise of our God.
Many shall see and fear
and shall trust in the LORD.—℟.

Blessed the man who has placed
his trust in the LORD,
and has not gone over to the proud
who follow false gods.—℟.

How many are the wonders and designs
that you have worked for us, O LORD my God;
you have no equal.
Should I wish to proclaim or speak of them,
they would be more than I can tell!—℟.

You delight not in sacrifice and offering,
but in an open ear.
You do not ask for holocaust and sin offering.—℟.

Then I said, "Behold, I have come."
In the scroll of the book it stands written of me:
"I delight to do your will, O my God;
your instruction lies deep within me."—℟.

56. b) Prayer

O God, who call us from darkness into your light,
from falsehood into truth,
from death into life,
pour your Holy Spirit into us,
to open our ears and strengthen our hearts,
that we may hear your call
and walk boldly in the way
that truly leads to the Christian life.
Through Christ our Lord.

℟. Amen.

57. c) Readings

FIRST READING Rom 7:18-25

1

A reading from the Letter of Saint Paul to the Romans

Brothers and sisters:
I know that good does not dwell in me, that is, in my flesh.
The willing is ready at hand, but doing the good is not.
For I do not do the good I want,
but I do the evil I do not want.

Now if I do what I do not want, it is no longer I who do it,
but sin that dwells in me.
So, then, I discover the principle
that when I want to do right, evil is at hand.
For I take delight in the law of God, in my inner self,
but I see in my members another principle
at war with the law of my mind,
taking me captive to the law of sin that dwells in my members.
Miserable one that I am!
Who will deliver me from this mortal body?
Thanks be to God through Jesus Christ our Lord.
Therefore, I myself, with my mind, serve the law of God
but, with my flesh, the law of sin.

The word of the Lord.

2

Rom 8:19-23

A reading from the Letter of Saint Paul to the Romans

Brothers and sisters:
Creation awaits with eager expectation
the revelation of the children of God;
for creation was made subject to futility,
not of its own accord but because of the one who subjected it,
in hope that creation itself
would be set free from slavery to corruption
and share in the glorious freedom of the children of God.
We know that all creation is groaning in labor pains even until now;
and not only that, but we ourselves,

who have the firstfruits of the Spirit,
we also groan within ourselves
as we wait for adoption, the redemption of our bodies.

The word of the Lord.

A liturgical song is sung, or a brief period of silence is observed.

GOSPEL

Mt 13:44-46

✠ A reading from the holy Gospel according to Matthew

Jesus said to his disciples:
"The Kingdom of heaven is like a treasure buried in a field,
which a person finds and hides again,
and out of joy goes and sells all that he has and buys that field.
Again, the Kingdom of heaven is like a merchant
searching for fine pearls.
When he finds a pearl of great price,
he goes and sells all that he has and buys it."

The Gospel of the Lord.

---

58. d) Homily

The Homily may address:

—the law of sin, which in us struggles against God;

—the necessity of giving up the way of sin, so that we may enter the Kingdom of God.

59. e) Examination of Conscience

After the Homily, the examination of conscience takes place; a sample text is found in Appendix III, p. 348. A period of silence should always be included, so that each person may examine his (her) conscience in a more personal manner.

60. f) Penitential Act

Christ the Lord has called sinners
into the Kingdom of his Father.
So, let each of us now
make a heartfelt act of contrition
with a firm purpose of amendment.

After a brief period of silence, all recite together:

I confess to almighty God
and to you, my brothers and sisters,
that I have greatly sinned,
in my thoughts and in my words,
in what I have done
and in what I have failed to do,

And, striking their breast, they say:

through my fault, through my fault,
through my most grievous fault;

Then they continue:

therefore I ask blessed Mary, ever-Virgin,
all the Angels and Saints,
and you, my brothers and sisters,
to pray for me to the Lord our God.

Minister:

Lord God, you know all things,
you know that we have a sincere intention
to better serve you
and our brothers and sisters.
Look upon us and hear our prayers.

Reader:

Give us the grace of true conversion.

℟. Lord, we ask you, hear our prayer.

Stir up in us the spirit of repentance
and confirm our purpose of amendment.

℟. Lord, we ask you, hear our prayer.

Forgive our sins
and have mercy on our failings.

℟. Lord, we ask you, hear our prayer.

Fill our hearts
with a spirit of trust and generosity.

℟. Lord, we ask you, hear our prayer.

Make us faithful disciples of your Son
and living members of his Church.

℟. Lord, we ask you, hear our prayer.

Minister:

God does not wish the death of sinners,
but rather that they be converted and live.
In his kindness, may he accept
the admission of our sins
and grant his great mercy to us
who pray as his Son taught us:

All say together:

**Our Father, who art in heaven,
hallowed be thy name;
thy kingdom come,
thy will be done
on earth as it is in heaven.
Give us this day our daily bread,
and forgive us our trespasses,
as we forgive those who trespass against us;
and lead us not into temptation,
but deliver us from evil.**

61. The celebration ends with an appropriate liturgical song and the dismissal.

VI. For the Sick

62. According to the condition of the sick people and the suitability of the place, the minister goes to the sick, gathered in one room, or else he brings them together in a chapel or a church. The minister should adapt carefully the texts themselves and their number to the condition of those taking part. Since in most instances none of the sick will be able to perform the function of reader, the minister should, if possible, invite another person to carry out this function.

Theme

"The time of sickness is a time of grace"

63. a) The greeting may be given in these or similar words:

My dear friends,
the message of repentance Jesus preached
is good news:
news, indeed, of the love and mercy of God,
who enables us to direct our whole life,
again and again, towards him.
Repentance therefore is a gift of God
to be received with a grateful heart.
With this in mind,
let us now open our consciences to God,
in great simplicity and humility,
and seek reconciliation from him,
as we forgive one another our trespasses.

If possible, a penitential song is sung at this point with the sick people, or even by a choir, if one is present.

64. b) Prayer

O God, fount of all goodness
and compassion,
give to your children,
gathered in your name,
a spirit of repentance and of trust,
that, as we seek forgiveness from you
and from our brothers and sisters,
we may sincerely confess our sins.
Renew, we pray, through this celebration,
our communion with you
and with our neighbor,
so that we may have strength
to serve you better.
Through Christ our Lord.

℟. Amen.

65. c) Readings

The readings may be introduced in these or similar words:

When we enjoy health
and other good things,
often we do not appreciate them
and lack gratitude.
In time of sickness, however,
we come to realize what a great gift
all these things are,
and without them, we easily lose heart.
God permits sickness,
so that our faith may be tested;
indeed, our suffering joined
to the sufferings of Christ
can be of great worth to us
and to the Church of God.
So a time of sickness is not useless
or utterly devoid of meaning,
but for those who accept it
with a right disposition
it truly becomes a time of grace.
Our celebration seeks
to increase this disposition.
For this reason we listen to the word of God,
examine our consciences,
and pour forth our prayers.

66.

FIRST READING Jas 5:13-16

A reading from the Letter of Saint James

Beloved:
Is anyone among you suffering?

He should pray.
Is anyone in good spirits?
He should sing a song of praise.
Is anyone among you sick?
He should summon the presbyters of the Church,
and they should pray over him
and anoint him with oil in the name of the Lord.
The prayer of faith will save the sick person,
and the Lord will raise him up.
If he has committed any sins, he will be forgiven.

Therefore, confess your sins to one another
and pray for one another, that you may be healed.
The fervent prayer of a righteous person is very powerful.

The word of the Lord.

RESPONSORIAL PSALM

Between the readings, a Psalm may be said or sung alternately, for example, Psalm 130 (129) (no. 145) or Psalm 51 (50) (no. 139).

GOSPEL

Mk 2:1-12

✠ A reading from the holy Gospel according to Mark

When Jesus returned to Capernaum after some days,
it became known that he was at home.
Many gathered together so that there was no longer room for them,
not even around the door,
and he preached the word to them.
They came bringing to him a paralytic carried by four men.
Unable to get near Jesus because of the crowd,
they opened up the roof above him.

After they had broken through,
they let down the mat on which the paralytic was lying.
When Jesus saw their faith, he said to him,
"Child, your sins are forgiven."
Now some of the scribes were sitting there asking themselves,
"Why does this man speak that way? He is blaspheming.
Who but God alone can forgive sins?"
Jesus immediately knew in his mind what
they were thinking to themselves,
so he said, "Why are you thinking such things in your hearts?
Which is easier, to say to the paralytic,
'Your sins are forgiven,'
or to say, 'Rise, pick up your mat and walk'?
But that you may know
that the Son of Man has authority to forgive sins on earth"
—he said to the paralytic,
"I say to you, rise, pick up your mat, and go home."
He rose, picked up his mat at once,
and went away in the sight of everyone.
They were all astounded
and glorified God, saying, "We have never seen anything like this."

The Gospel of the Lord.

---

67. d) Homily

It is appropriate that the celebrant speak of sickness, dwelling not so much on sickness of the body as on the failings of the soul. He should emphasize the power of Jesus and his Church to forgive sins and the power of suffering offered vicariously for others.

68. e) Examination of Conscience

After the Homily, the examination of conscience takes place; a sample text is found in Appendix III, p. 348. A period of silence should always be included, so that each person may examine his (her) conscience in a more personal manner.

The following questions may be added but adapted to the condition of the sick:

—Do I trust in the goodness
and providence of God
even in times of affliction and sickness?

—Do I dwell on my sickness
and indulge in despair
and other harmful thoughts and feelings?

—Do I use my quiet moments
to reflect on my life
and my relationship with God?

—Do I accept sickness and pain
as opportunities to suffer with Christ,
who redeemed us by his suffering?

—Living by faith,
am I convinced that pain
borne with patience
brings great good to the Church?

—Am I attentive to others
and respectful of my fellow-sufferers
and their needs?

—Am I grateful for those who care for me and those who visit me?

—Am I careful to show a good example, as befits a Christian?

**—Am I sorry for my past sins,
and do I bear my sickness
and infirmity patiently to atone for them?**

69. f) Penitential Act

After a moment of silence, all recite together:

I confess to almighty God
and to you, my brothers and sisters,
that I have greatly sinned,
in my thoughts and in my words,
in what I have done
and in what I have failed to do,

And, striking their breast, they say:

through my fault, through my fault,
through my most grievous fault;

Then they continue:

therefore I ask blessed Mary, ever-Virgin,
all the Angels and Saints,
and you, my brothers and sisters,
to pray for me to the Lord our God.

Lector:

**Lord our God, we bear the name
of your Son and we call you our Father.
We are sorry we have offended you
and wronged our brothers and sisters.**

℟. Grant us true repentance and stir up in us love for you and our neighbor.

Lord Jesus Christ,
by your Passion and Cross
you have redeemed us and given us
an example of patience and love.
We are sorry we have offended you
and neglected to serve you
and our brothers and sisters.

℟. Grant us true repentance and stir up in us love for you and our neighbor.

Lord, Holy Spirit, you speak to us
in the Church and in our conscience,
rousing our hearts to do good.
We are sorry we have offended you
by disobedience and hardness of heart.

℟. Grant us true repentance and stir up in us love for you and our neighbor.

Minister:

Let us now turn to God our Father in prayer,
that he may forgive us our sins
and deliver us from evil:

Our Father, who art in heaven,
hallowed be thy name;
thy kingdom come,
thy will be done
on earth as it is in heaven.
Give us this day our daily bread,
and forgive us our trespasses,

as we forgive those who trespass against us;
and lead us not into temptation,
but deliver us from evil.

70. Then, if appropriate, the choir or the assembled faithful may sing a liturgical song, and the celebration concludes with a prayer of thanksgiving:

71.

God of consolation and Father of mercies,
who forgive the sins of those
who confess to you:

℟. We praise you and we bless you.

God of consolation and Father of mercies,
who grant the afflicted and those in pain
a share in the Passion of your Son
for the salvation of all the world:

℟. We praise you and we bless you.

God of consolation and Father of mercies,
who love the distressed
and those who mourn,
giving them the hope of salvation
and promising them
the reward of eternal life:

℟. We praise you and we bless you.

Let us pray.

Your goodness, Lord, is without measure
and your mercy without end.
We give you thanks for the gifts
we have received.

Look, we pray, upon this your family
gathered in the name of your Son
and preserve in them
a living faith, firm hope,
and sincere charity toward you
and their neighbor.
Through Christ our Lord.

℟. Amen.

Or:

72. In place of the prayer, the celebration may conclude with a blessing:

May the God of peace fill your hearts
with every good thing,
that strengthened by divine hope
and consolation
and living according to his will,
you may attain to eternal salvation.
May almighty God bestow upon you these
and all good things:
the Father, and the Son, ✠
and the Holy Spirit.

℟. Amen.

73. The minister dismisses the assembly, or invites those present to a friendly visit with the sick.

APPENDIX III

FORM FOR THE EXAMINATION OF CONSCIENCE

1. This form is proposed for the examination of conscience, to be completed and adapted according to local usages and the needs of different individuals.

---

2. When an examination of conscience is made before the Sacrament of Penance, it is appropriate that each should ask himself (herself) the following questions before all others:

1. Do I come to the Sacrament of Penance with a sincere desire for purification, conversion, renewal of life, and deeper friendship with God, or do I consider it rather as a burden to be undertaken as seldom as possible?

2. Did I forget, or deliberately fail to mention, any grave sins in previous confessions?

3. Have I performed the penance imposed on me? Have I made reparation for injuries committed? Have I put into practice the purpose of amendment of life, according to the Gospel?

---

3. In the light of the word of God, each individual should examine his (her) life.

I. The Lord says: "You shall love the Lord your God with all your heart" (Mt 22:37).

1. Is my heart directed to God, so that I truly love him above all things by the faithful keeping of his commandments, as a son loves his father, or am I more concerned with worldly matters? Do I have a right intention in what I do?

2. Do I have firm faith in God, who has spoken to us through his Son? Have I adhered firmly to the teaching of the Church? Have I taken care to be instructed in the Christian faith, listening to the word of God, participating in catechesis, avoiding things harmful to the faith? Have I always professed my faith in God and the Church boldly, without fear? Have I been willing to be known as a Christian in my private and public life?

3. Have I said my morning and evening prayers, or not? Is my prayer a true conversation with God, in mind and heart, or merely an exterior observance? Have I offered to God my difficulties, my joys, and my sorrows? Do I turn to him in temptations?

4. Do I have reverence and love for God's name, or have I offended God by blasphemy, by swearing falsely, or by taking his name in vain? Have I been irreverent to the Blessed Virgin Mary or to the Saints?

5. Do I keep the Lord's Day and the feasts of the Church by actively, reverently, and attentively participating in public worship, especially the Mass? Have I obeyed the precept of annual confession and Communion at Easter?

6. Do I perhaps have other gods, that is to say, things for which I care more, or in which I trust more than God, such as money, superstitions, spirit-worship, or other occult practices?

II. The Lord says: "This is my commandment, that you love one another as I have loved you" (Jn 15:12).

1. Do I have a genuine love for my neighbor, or do I misuse them for my own ends, or do to them what I do not wish to be done to me by others? Have I given grave scandal to them by my words and actions?

2. Consider whether, within your family, you have contributed to the good and joy of others through patience and genuine love, whether as children you have been obedient to your parents, showing them honor and offering them help in their spiritual and material needs; or whether, as parents, you have been careful to bring your children up in the Christian faith, helping them by good example and parental discipline; or as spouses, you have been faithful to one another in your hearts and in your dealings with others?

3. Do I share my goods with others who are poorer than myself? As far as I can, do I defend the oppressed, comfort the sorrowful, help those in need, or have I despised my neighbor, especially the poor, the frail, the old, strangers, and people of a different race?

4. Am I mindful, in my life, of the mission I received at my Confirmation? Have I taken part in the apostolic and charitable works of the Church and in the life of the parish? Have I helped to meet the needs of the Church and prayed for them, e.g., for the unity of the Church, for the evangelization of peoples, for peace and justice, etc.?

5. Am I concerned for the good and prosperity of the human community in which I live, or do I spend my life caring only for myself? Do I take part, to the best of my ability, in promoting justice, morality, concord, and charity in human society? Have I done my civic duty? Have I paid my taxes?

6. In my work or profession am I just, industrious, honest, offering my services to society out of love? Have I given a fair wage to my employees and those who serve me? Have I kept my promises and contracts?

7. Have I obeyed the lawful authorities and shown them due respect?

8. If I am in a position of responsibility or authority, do I use it for my own benefit or for the good of others, in a spirit of service?

9. Have I been truthful and faithful, or have I done harm to others by lies, calumny, detraction, rash judgment, or breaking confidentiality?

10. Have I violated the life, physical health, reputation or honor, or goods of others? Have I caused them any loss? Have I advised or procured an abortion? Have I fostered hatred towards others? Have I cut myself off from others through quarrels, enmity, insults, or anger? Have I, through culpable selfishness, neglected to bear witness to the innocence of my neighbor?

11. Have I stolen things that do not belong to me? Have I unjustly and inordinately desired them or damaged them? Have I made restitution of stolen goods and reparation for damage?

12. If I have suffered injuries, have I been ready, for the love of Christ, to grant peace and forgiveness, or do I harbor hatred and the desire for revenge?

III. Christ the Lord says: "Whoever has my commandments and observes them is the one who loves me" (Jn 14:21).

1. What is the fundamental motivating force of my life? Am I inspired by the hope of eternal life? Have I tried to grow in the spiritual life by prayer, by listening to and meditating on the word of God, by partaking in the Sacraments, by self-denial? Have I tried to control my vices, my evil passions and inclinations, such as envy or the love of food and drink? Have I, motivated by pride and boastfulness, exalted myself in the sight of God and had contempt for others, considering myself better than them? Have I imposed my will on others, not respecting the liberty and rights of others?

2. What use have I made of my time, of my powers, of the gifts which I have received from God like the talents of the Gospel? Do I use these things to make myself more perfect day by day? Have I been lazy and slothful?

3. Have I borne the sorrows and difficulties of life patiently? To what extent have I disciplined myself so as to "make up those things which are lacking in the Passion of Christ"? Have I kept the law of fasting and abstinence?

4. Have I preserved my senses and my whole body in purity and chastity as a temple of the Holy Spirit destined for resurrection and glory and as a sign of the love which the faithful God has for his people, as is clearly manifest in the Sacrament of Matrimony? Have I debased my flesh by fornication, impurity, unworthy words and thoughts, or disordered desires or actions? Have I indulged my appetites? Have I indulged in readings, conversations, or watched things contrary to Christian and human decency? Have I incited others to sin by my own indecency? Have I kept the moral law in married life?

5. Have I acted contrary to my conscience through fear or hypocrisy?

6. Have I always tried to act truly in the freedom of the children of God, according to the law of the Spirit, or am I the slave of any passion?

ISBN 978-1-958237-09-0
90000
9 781958 237090